THOUGHTS

ON THE

DECALOGUE.

BY

HOWARD CROSBY,
PASTOR OF THE FOURTH AVENUE PRESBYTERIAN CHURCH,
NEW YORK.

PHILADELPHIA:
PRESBYTERIAN BOARD OF PUBLICATION,
1334 CHESTNUT STREET.

WESTCOTT & THOMSON,
Stereotypers and Electrotypers, Phila.

CONTENTS.

Thoughts on the Decalogue.

The Preamble.

I am the Lord thy God, which have brought thee out of the land of Egypt, out of the house of bondage.—Exodus xx. 2.

GOD has several times spoken directly to men without the agency of inspiration, using some power in nature other than a rational medium. Thus has he spoken to Moses, to Elijah and Job, to the apostles on the Mount of Transfiguration, and to Paul near Damascus.

But although God has thus frequently *spoken* to men, he has but once *written* a message to his creatures. The Decalogue stands alone as God's *manuscript*. Of it it is said, "The Lord said unto Moses,

'Come up to me in the mount and be there, and I will give thee tables of stone and a law and commandments (that is, a law of commandments) *which I have written,*'" and then afterward it is said, "And he gave unto Moses, when he had made an end of communing with him upon Mount Sinai, two tables of testimony, *written with the finger of God.*"

Still again it is said, "And Moses turned and went down from the mount, and the two tables of the testimony were in his hand: the tables were written on both their sides; on the one side and on the other were they written. And the tables were the work of God, *and the writing was the writing of God*, graven upon the tables."

These are the accounts in the Book of Exodus. Afterward, in Deuteronomy, Moses recapitulates to Israel God's ways with them, and then, at the close of their desert life of forty years, the venerable leader of Israel says of the scene at Sinai,

"The Lord spake with you out of the midst of the fire; ye heard the voice of the words, but saw no similitude; only ye heard a voice, and he declared unto you his covenant, which he commanded you to perform, even ten commandments; and *he wrote them upon* two tables of stone." Then, after repeating the ten commandments, he says, "These words the Lord spake unto all your assembly in the mount out of the midst of the fire, of the cloud and of the thick darkness, with a great voice, and he added no more; and *he wrote them* in two tables of stone and delivered them unto me."

These tables thus prepared were broken by Moses beneath the mount under a righteous impulse of indignation at Israel's fearful sin. But he was again called up to the top of Sinai, and the order he received is thus given by Moses himself:

"At that time the Lord said unto me, 'Hew thee two tables of stone like unto the first, and come up unto me into the mount, . . . and *I will write on the tables* the words that were in the first tables which thou brakest; . . . and I hewed two tables of stone like unto the first, and went up into the mount, having the two tables in my hand; and *he wrote on the tables*, according to the first writing, *the ten commandments*."

So these second tables, which were preserved in the ark nearly a thousand years, although they were not themselves prepared by God, as were the first, but were hewn by the hand of Moses, bore, nevertheless, as much as did the first, the autograph of the Almighty. It is this fact which exalts the Decalogue to the very highest rank of all recorded truth. It must be truth of the highest importance to man that receives so distinguishing a mark at the hand of God. We cannot restrict its application to a single people, a single locality or a single age. The thunderings and lightnings, the trumpet-noise and smoking mountain, formed a fitting framework for the divine speech, and indicated the limits of humanity to be the sole limits of its application. The rest of the law given to Israel had none of this awful majesty of publishment. All the details of ceremonial service and civil order were given to the people through the mediation of Moses, spoken by him and recorded by him. They were evidently intended for a special nation and a limited period, and it is they of which Paul speaks in the Epistle to the Galatians, when he says that "the law was added (or attached) because of transgressions, till the seed should come to whom the promise was made; and it was ordained by angels in the hand of a mediator;" for the *Decalogue* did not pass from God through either angels or mediator, but came direct from God to all Israel.

It becomes us, then, to study with deep reverence these words so remarkably given —these spiritual aerolites that sought our earth directly from the upper world.

We find, at the very first glance, that they are exceedingly simple. Every one can readily receive and understand them—they have relation to human action in spheres where human action is universally found. They are therefore exceedingly practical, though by no means merely of outward force. They relate to the action of the heart as of the life. Loving, honoring and serving are enjoined, which directly regard the affections.

It is a common misapprehension of the ten commandments to restrict their meaning to overt action—to the visible life. The rich young ruler who came to Jesus with such animation, and went away so sorrowful, made this mistake. God's law is not, like man's law, a mere recognizer of the overt and visible, but touches the whole man, and is therefore specially concerned with the inner springs of life. It sees the whole value of the outward activity to be in the condition of the soul, and hence the apostle, in terse apophthegm, says, "Love is the fulfilling of the law," and hence our Saviour translates the whole Decalogue thus, using the very words of Moses, and using, too, a formula known to the Jewish people: "Thou shalt love the Lord thy God with all thy heart and with all thy soul, with all thy mind and with all thy strength; . . . Thou shalt love thy neighbor as thyself."

Thus we see four characteristics of these wonderful commandments: first, their universality; secondly, their simplicity; thirdly, their practicalness; and fourthly, their spirituality.

In regard to their structure and analysis, they consist of ten distinct precepts and a preface. Let us look at the preface before we examine the first precept.

"*I am the Lord thy God, which have brought thee out of the land of Egypt, out of the house of bondage.*"

Bearing in mind the universality of the Decalogue, this "land of Egypt" and "house of bondage" must have a far deeper and wider signification than the Valley of the Nile. We find, from other parts of Scripture, that the land of Egypt, from its peculiar relation to God's ancient people, became typical and emblematic of that which might be oppressive and inimical to the truth. For example, the great city which destroys the witnesses, or rather holds their dead bodies unburied, as given in the Apocalypse, is called "Egypt." Rev. xi. 8. So again, when the prophet Zechariah makes use of the name in the following passage, he evidently does not intend the literal Egypt, which had already lost its independence: "I will bring them again also out of the land of Egypt, and gather them out of Assyria, and the pride of Assyria shall be brought down, and the sceptre of Egypt shall depart away." When the prophet uttered this, Egypt had no sceptre, and Assyria no existence as a nation; and we are forced to one of two interpretations, either a *literal one* which implies that Egypt shall be again resuscitated as an independent empire and Israel again dwell therein, and that Assyria shall be again resuscitated as an independent empire and Israel again be captive therein, or the figurative one which points to God's spiritual Israel in a spiritual captivity to a spiritual Egypt.

If it be asked which is to be accepted as the true interpretation, I cannot see any ground for the literal. I believe that both here and elsewhere in the Prophets Egypt is a synonym for an ungodly world, which captivates the heart of man, and from which the grace of God releases the renewed soul.

The law of God is, therefore, in its holiness, justice and goodness, held up to those who have been delivered from the bondage of sin—those who have been released from the spiritual Egypt. It is not so held up to the ungodly—they cannot love it, they cannot see its beauty. The law of God is given us as a rule of life, not as a means of salvation. By the Lord's telling us that he has already brought us out of Egypt and bondage, he does not say when he gives us the law, "Do this and live," but, "Since ye live, do this;" "Since my grace has redeemed you, and you rejoice in the liberty of the children of God, use my law, the reflection of my perfections, as your beloved guide."

This is the position of the Decalogue to us. It is not addressed to the unconverted, save as a condemning law. All the message given to them is, "Be reconciled to God." When they look at the law, they see what does not belong to them, and so see it all awry, and they read it, "Do this and live," instead of, "Live and do this." Thus they get themselves into a great deal of trouble in trying to work out a holy life from unholy material, sometimes deceiving themselves into thoughts of success, and sometimes giving way to a despair which is very legitimate from their premises. No; we cannot repeat it too often that the law *in its love and obedience* is only for God's Israel; for the rest it is simply a monument of condemnation, a token that they are unholy and cannot keep it.

The law comes before the gospel historically and logically, but the gospel comes before the law biographically and practically. The law is the token and standard of holiness, but the gospel is the gate to that holiness.

We are saved by the free grace of God which the Gospel proclaims—we are saved by simply letting Christ save us, by appropriating his precious promises, by *doing nothing*, but by *believing; then, after* that salvation, we are shown the holy, just and good law of God as our rule of life, our pattern of holiness; and the new nature, which we have through faith in Christ, is able to appreciate and obey it with more or less perfectness, according to our amount of faith and sanctification. The greater our faith, the greater both our obedience *to* and our love *of* the Decalogue. In the triumphs of an exalted faith, we say with David, "My soul hath kept thy testimonies, and I love them exceedingly."

There is another portion of the preface to the law which points to this same exclusive application of the law to the people of God. It is this, "I am the Lord thy God," or, literally, "I am Jehovah, thy God." The word "Jehovah" designates, not God the creator and general governor, not God the all-powerful, all-wise, all-knowing and omnipresent, not God in his essential excellence and character, but God the lover and redeemer of his people, God who promises and brings salvation, God in his special relation to his own faithful ones. When he delivered Israel from Egypt, God first practically disclosed this name as his name to his Israel. Of it he says himself to Moses, when the exodus was about to take place, "I am Jehovah; and I appeared unto Abraham, unto Isaac and unto Jacob, by the name of El Shaddai (God Almighty), but by my name Jehovah was I not known to them; . . . and *ye* shall know that I am *Jehovah* your God which bringeth you out from under the burdens of the Egyptians." Now, the Decalogue is given to those who can call God "Jehovah *our* God," our special Saviour and Deliverer from sin, and to none else. Let this not be misunderstood. I am not excusing any sinner from the condemnation of disobedience and sin. They are all invited to make God "Jehovah *their* God," and for rejecting that invitation they must suffer the just results of their depravity and sin. But it is only when the heart recognizes Jehovah as its own God, when it comes over and joins the true Israel, that the law can be operative in it. The efficiency of the law as a rule of life is built on the faith which accepts God as the deliverer from sin's bondage. The law is a holy thing, and nobody has anything to do with it but those who are made holy in Christ. Therefore, unconverted sinners, seek Christ, if you want to keep the law; you can only reach the law through him.

There is one other expression in this preface which should be noted. It is the use of the second person singular, "which have brought *thee* out of the land of Egypt." There are two thoughts connected with this use. The first is that *God deals with all Israel as one man.* He expects them to be one, of one mind and one heart, before him. There must be no antagonisms among God's people. Bickerings, whether ecclesiastical or private, have no place in the Church of our Redeemer. They are Satans in the camp, adversaries to be excluded and destroyed. There are twelve encampments with twelve standards, but there is only one tabernacle and only one Moses, and the twelve tribes unite as one family and march in harmonious ranks. If Christians differ in taste and outward name, it is well; but if they mark their difference by bitterness and hostility to any degree, they are destroying the unity of the Spirit, which is only maintained by the bond of peace. Superciliousness, censoriousness, coldness between Christians of whatever name or names, are as inimical to Christian unity as are open contention and calumny. The latter may be more conspicuous and make more immediate trouble, but the former are just as devilish in their origin and texture, and their results are perhaps even more fatal by reason of their more secret working. There is one bond which should bind all believers together—the love of the common Master; and in this love all differences should sink to nothing, or, at most, become mere harmless theories. He has taken us out of the contentious world, not that we should be only another contentious world, but that we should show on distracted earth the harmony of heaven. He wishes to *reconcile* all things unto himself. He is our peace, who hath made Jew and

Gentile, men the most opposite in view and feeling, *one*. Sin divides men, grace unites them.

The other thought regarding the use of the second person singular here is this: *God treats man individually*. Man enters heaven or hell, not in companies or battalions, but in naked individuality. Sin is personal, condemnation is personal, salvation is personal. Social sin and social morality are delusions, or, at least, figurative phrases. Society has no conscience, heart or purpose; it only has a history. It is the individual alone who has the moral attributes, and who makes society and social history. In this way I see that God's law comes directly to me—not to me as a member of society, but to me as an individual man, with a heart and conscience, which heart and conscience the law would fit, if there were no society on the face of the earth. You, my Christian reader, are as personally addressed by God in this holy law as if the entire Church of Christ consisted of you alone. "That brought *thee* out of the land of Egypt." It was thyself personally that wert delivered from that dark Egypt of condemnation, was it not? It was thyself personally that received the benefit of Christ's paschal death, was it not? And so you can say, "Who loved *me* and gave himself for *me*."

And now, shall the holy gospel concentrate its beauty all on your own single self, and the holy law be denied an equal concentration with its equal beauty? No, no! Jesus, when he *redeemed* you, meant to *sanctify* you. The gospel was his means, but the law was his end. It is his own gospel and his own law; and just as his love is personal to you, so are both gospel and law (the one the expression of *his* love, the other the summons to *your* love) personal to you. When we can say, "I am my Beloved's, and my Beloved is mine," I'm sure we can say, too, "Oh how love I thy law!"

My unrenewed reader, if this law is not

for you, because you are not adapted to it, it is a witness against you through that non-adaptation. God has offered to put you in relation with that law through the gospel, and your non-acceptance of the divine grace is a witness of the deep power of sin in your heart. God's voice of offer, and God's voice of condemnation, are as personal to you as his giving of the law is personal to every follower of Christ. They are as personal to you as if God and you stood alone in the universe. God recognizes only the individual. "Thou art the man," is his judgment. Your sin is personal—you know it; your condemnation is personal, fearfully personal. May you know that, so as to make your salvation personal in our Lord Jesus Christ!

THE FIRST COMMANDMENT.

"*Thou shalt have no other gods before me.*"—EXODUS xx. 3.

WE have noted that the Decalogue was universal in its application, and simple, practical, and spiritual in its character. We have also noted that its preface teaches—(1) that it can only be appreciated and honored by God's own people, and (2) that God deals with each man separately, and with his own people as made one in Christ. We now enter upon the consideration of the first of the ten commandments:

"*Thou shalt have no other gods before me.*"

"Before me" is "in my presence;" and as Jehovah is everywhere present, it means "anywhere." Wherever a god is set up in the entire universe, it is set up in the presence of Jehovah. The idea of God in the human mind involves the notion of a supreme being who is governor of all, and to whom is due the homage of all. Even polytheism has to place over its many subordinate gods *one* thus supreme. It is an intuitive demand of the mind. Now, the mere making and using of a wooden or stone idol to represent a god is, we see at a glance, by no means requisite in order that the soul shall subjectively have such a god. The outward statue is perfectly harmless in itself, and is only dangerous as connected with the ideal god represented by it and supposed to be mysteriously united to it. This commandment really has nothing to do with the subject of gross heathen idolatry, the use and worship of visible idols. The *second* commandment looks in that direction, but this takes higher ground and calls the soul to the contemplation of first principles. It might be read in the singular, "Thou shalt have no other god before me," and I believe that is the more correct way of reading the word "Elohim" in this passage. It declares that Jehovah will have no rival for supreme homage—that the heart of man shall recognize none but himself as God and guide. The reasons are embodied in the phrase "before me." Any such rivalry would be an insult to Jehovah's majesty. It would be like introducing a usurper into the king's throne-room and there offering him allegiance. It would be a tacit declaration that Jehovah was not competent to govern his creation alone, but must give over some of his provinces to others who would manage their affairs, and thus relieve him. Of course this embraces in its condemnation both the polytheism of paganism and the semi-polytheism of Romanism, but its main and primary charge has relation to the general abandonment of Jehovah by the human heart.

Two thoughts here suggest themselves:

I. *All want of a positive allegiance to Jehovah is a positive allegiance to another Elohim or supreme God.*

A self-reliant man, in the strict sense of the word, never yet existed. Man's nature is such that he looks without him for support, as the ivy feels for the tree or the wall. We use the phrase "a self-reliant man" of one who stands independent of his fellow-man, but he is not independent of *some* outer prop. He has a god. If he had not, he would be himself a god. If he has not the true and living God as his stay, then he is an idolater. Because he has no outward idol, no painted or sculptured work of art before which he bows, his idolatry is probably the more inveterate, because the more hidden and deceptive, unperceived by himself. He follows his master, he concentrates his energies in his service, and is yet ready to deny the obvious relation which these facts imply. It is this gross deception which is hiding the precipice from many a careless soul. Some of my readers, it may be, are wrapt in this mist, supposing that Jehovah is their God, but forgetting that "covetousness is idolatry."

God's will concerning you, his purpose in regard to his own eternal kingdom, his word, his Church, his love,—these were never known to you as objects of desire or motives of action. You have lived a score or scores of years upon this earth, and yet never inquired, "What are the commands of God who put me here?" Have you been idle? Have you been asleep? By no means. You have been active and wide awake every day. In your business or profession you have worked with a will. You have therefore had *motives*, for man cannot work without motives, and you have had a *supreme motive*, for one motive must in practice control all others, for all action is the result of the dominant motive that has either crushed the others or brought them along in its train. Now, has a regard for God been your dominant motive, or even any *one* of your motives, as you formed your plans or proceeded to their execution?

You have no hesitation in answering my question. God has not been in all your thoughts—that is, as a power. You have had an intellectual apprehension of the true God—you have even, at times, been agitated in your emotional nature with the idea of the Almighty; but this intelligence and transient sensation have not had to do with the working-force of your being. Yet you have had a supreme motive. What, then, has it been? Was it the desire for wealth? or for rank or position? or for social appreciation? or for intellectual greatness? or for worldly ease and pleasure? Whichever it was, here is your god, your Elohim, the governor and guide of your life, to which the real homage of your heart is given. You lean upon it as your ultimate good. Your life is arranged with a single view to its attainment. You measure everything by this standard. You have been so accustomed to this for years that you are perhaps yourself unconscious of the processes of your devotion. You do not stop to analyze the motives of an activity that has almost become an instinct. But now I ask you honestly to consider whether this be not your god, by no figure of speech, but in plainest reality. What worship could you render more devout than that of your affections? Surely the mere outward kneeling and oral praying do not form the soul of worship. They are the mere dress of a true homage. We know well that in the high spiritual sense in which all these things are to be regarded by immortal spirits, and in which they *are* regarded by the infinite God, *the heart in its attachments* forms the real life, the actual worship, of the man. That heart of yours has no attachment to the true and living God, and yet it *has* its attachment, its controlling attachment; it could not live a moment without one.

Now, special pleading aside, is it not clear that you are deliberately breaking the first and root commandment of God's written law, "Thou shalt have no other god before me"? Have you not another god, just as truly in the estimation of all spiritual intelligences as if you kneeled daily to a statue of Jupiter or Baal in your parlor? All those applications for wisdom and help, all those ascriptions of gladness and gratitude, all those movements of regard and consideration which belong to your almighty Creator and Benefactor, are bestowed elsewhere, and whither they go, there is your god. Your whole being gravitates directly away from the true God by this positive action of your will and affections.

As test questions of this condition of your being, let me offer you these. Use them candidly, and see where their consideration brings you:

1. Have I ever loved God's word and made it my counselor?

2. Have I found prayer to God a relief and source of strength?

3. Have I identified myself with God's people?

4. Have I dwelt hopefully upon the blessings provided in God's heavenly and eternal kingdom?

5. Has my heart been grieved that I did not love and serve my God better?

These questions probe your heart. You cannot say "Yes" to any one of them. The conclusion your intellect can appreciate, though not your heart—that *God is not your God*, and hence that you are an idolater.

In the quiet hours of the Sabbath, given to you for just such opportunities, deal faithfully with yourself and ponder on all these things. Look at the past and at the future. Think of what you have been, and what you ought to be. Consider alike the reproach and the peril of a position aloof from God while in the midst of God's universe, with every pulsation of your being his gift, and surrounded by the appeals of his infinite love. In your retirement meet the question fairly; throw aside all metaphysical subtleties about destiny and nature, and say out boldly what you know: "I have rejected God—I have chosen other gods—I have acted as independently and deliberately as if I were the sole being in the universe; I *wish* to follow other gods than Jehovah. I love these other gods; they please and excite me, and in this excitement I lose sight of all those unpleasant questions about eternity and righteousness and justice which are so hateful to my soul."

Ah, when you say all that truth plainly to yourself, will you not shudder at the position it reveals? In this path of honest dealing with yourself is your only safety.

II. *All allegiance to God that does not recognize him as he has revealed himself is allegiance to a false god.*

God has shown himself to us, we may say, in the face of outward nature and in the inward nature of our minds. But both these natural sources have been corrupted. Sin has so disarranged our faculties as to make our contemplation both of the material and the spiritual creation very defective and deformed. All sorts of conflicting theories have grown up to deceive the mind and ruin the heart from these injured germs. As pure and sinless, we should have seen truth reflected both from our own souls and from every hill and valley of our earth. Each thought would have been a revelation, and each star a shining wisdom. But wrecked as we are by sin, these means are no longer effective. We have gone off and learned to speak a barbarous tongue, and the language of God's creation we cannot understand. A new revelation—a revelation to *sinners*—must be made, as God's love yearns to call us back to salvation and holiness, and this revelation is made in the written word. Here the goodness of the sin-pardoning God is disclosed; nature could never have taught *that.* Here the sympathy and atonement of God as man are discovered; nature could never have taught *that.* In short, here, and here only, is the way back to God and purity and bliss revealed for us wandering and lost sinners. Now, the only true idea of God can be found in this heavenly record. The gospel view of God is of one who is infinitely holy and just, and who cannot regard sin ("of purer eyes than to behold evil and canst not look on iniquity"), and yet who can be just while he justifies the sinner who believes in Jesus.

The gospel view of God represents him as in covenant with all such believers (and with none else), giving them his full pardon, and implanting in them a true holiness. To them he is Jehovah, the covenant-making and covenant-keeping God, and Jesus is the mediator of this covenant. Jesus is our peace and righteousness. Through his sacrifice in our behalf, justice no longer threatens us, and holiness visits our souls; and this wonderful change, from condemned sinners to honored saints, results altogether from our union with Jesus by faith and love. Eternal joy at God's right hand awaits those who are thus united, forgiven and sanctified. This is God as he has revealed himself. This is Jehovah, the God of his own dear people. Now, any idea of God as the universal Father (an idea founded on natural theology and human wishes), who regards all his creatures alike and will treat them all alike, and will see to it that they all alike reach eternal glory,—any such idea is foreign and opposed to this revelation, and any such god is a false god.

So a view of God as careless of personal holiness in his creatures or as too exalted to notice all their minute acts and thoughts, or as tyrannical and arbitrary in his dealings with them, or as appeasable by self-denials and penances, is a view of a false god, and not a view of Jehovah, the only living and true God. And the man who, despising or neglecting the Holy Scriptures, and trusting to his reason or his dreams or to nature or to nothing, holds such a god before his mind, is an idolater; he has put another Elohim before Jehovah Elohim. Because the thought of the divine Being which he thus introduces into his heart becomes the substitute for the *true* motion that should guide his life, he puts the helm into as false hands as if he had delivered it to Mammon. In truth, it will be found that this false god is only an image made up in the interests of Mammon and his train, and representing their demands upon the affections. The true God is shorn of all his glorious attributes in order that sin may be practiced, and thus is not the true God at all, and the soul flatters itself it is worshiping the true God, when it has enshrined worldliness.

In view of the two thoughts we have thus noted—(1) *that God must have a positive allegiance*, and (2) *that it must be yielded to God as he has revealed himself*, several subordinate thoughts naturally follow.

1. *The help of the true God, Jehovah-Jesus, should be sought by us to overthrow our false gods.* By that very act we should offer our rightful allegiance, and, in so doing, consecrate our life to the rightful service of Him who is our rightful king. We can never make head against our carnal gods by ourselves. They are too much like us, and we are too much like them, for any honest, persistent and successful opposition on our part. Just here Jehovah's help comes in. Introduce *his* ark, and Dagon will fall down and be shattered. The Almighty, who says, "Thou shalt have no other gods before me," says also to his Israel, who asks to be delivered from strange gods, "Against all the gods of Egypt I will execute judgment." It is to him you must cry as your conscience tells you and warns you of your folly in worshiping worldly gods.

"I am weak, but thou art mighty;
Guide me by thy powerful hand."

He will wrest our gods from us, and will pluck us from our gods, even if it cause pain; and if we are honest in asking his help, we shall be willing to endure the pain for the truth, the peace, the honor and the glory of serving the living and true God. Then to him I urge you, who have thus far followed other guides than Jehovah—to *him* I urge you to apply before opportunity is lost, and you and your gods find a common destruction.

2. *How watchful we should be in this earth, where the false gods are not only plenty, but exactly after the fashion of our own depraved hearts!* It was said of Athens that at each corner there was a new god, and some have even said that in population Athens had more gods than men. It is so with our unseen gods of the unregenerate heart. They abound with different names and different characters, according to the tastes and cha-

racters of different men. In this way there are actually more of these gods than of men. But there is only one Jehovah, and his character is unalterable. He cannot accommodate his perfections to the varied and depraved tastes of men. His purity is wholly contrary to their condition and aims. The heart is not, therefore, going to gravitate naturally into piety. It is not going to quit its dear earthly gods and fall before Jehovah in reverence and affection *as a matter of course.* It must arise to arms; it must assume its attitude of warfare; it must act as sentinel as well as combatant. It must suspect everything earthly as a seduction to sin, and only be satisfied when it has probed it with the sword of the Spirit, which is the word of God.

3. *The word of God ought to be in our hands all the while.* This is the only offensive weapon against our false gods. With it we can cut them to pieces, hip and thigh. The Scripture enlightens and purifies us.

To be sanctified though his word of truth is what Christ desires for his dear people. How we are rebuked by this thought! The Bible's collected dust testifies against us. The sword of the Spirit is covered with rust. We must love the word more, and to do this we must know it more and use it more. So only shall we be guiltless in regard to the first commandment of the law.

The Second Commandment.

"*Thou shalt not make unto thee any graven image, or any likeness of any thing that is in heaven above, or that is in the earth beneath, or that is in the water under the earth: thou shalt not bow down thyself to them, nor serve them: for I the Lord thy God am a jealous God, visiting the iniquity of the fathers upon the children unto the third and fourth generation of them that hate me; and showing mercy unto thousands of them that love me, and keep my commandments.*"—EXODUS xx. 4–6.

THE first commandment, as we have seen, is the prohibition of any supreme object of affection and reverence in the heart but Jehovah, or any dependence for the guidance of life other than on him. The second commandment has regard to one specific form of withdrawing the heart's allegiance from Jehovah—a form which has been most successful in its sad results, and which has seduced the vast majority of our race from the service of the true God. The first commandment forbids an *inward*, the second forbids an *outward*, idolatry.

We are not well situated to understand the fascinations of image-worship. Our peculiar type of civilization, largely moulded by a pure and spiritual Christianity, has in it a prejudice against the grossness of a god of stone or metal which renders the history of idolatry almost unintelligible. We are slow to imagine that a sensible man—a man of ordinary human wisdom—could bow down and pray to a sculptured deity; and yet we are met by the stubborn fact that the wisest of men (as far as *human* wisdom went) paid this adoring homage to the gods of Greece and Rome. It is not the tattooed savage and the degraded cannibal who monopolize this worship, but the poets, the philosophers, the statesmen, of the chosen land of art and science herein showed their kinsmanship to the Maories and the Feejees.

With all the careful training of the Jewish people, and although they were especially warned against this form of error, sin and ruin, they were charmed into its embrace, and filled the holy land with Baalim and Ashteroth, the male and female gods of the neighboring kingdoms. Solomon, their wisest king and wisest man, set the example, and the whole nation eagerly followed it. Against this most fatal style of sin the prophets inveighed with faithful vehemence; and for this supreme iniquity of the land, the nation was dragged behind the triumphal cars of Assyria and Babylon.

Let us hear Jeremiah as an example of the warning voices of the prophets:

"Hear ye the word of the Lord, O kings of Judah and inhabitants of Jerusalem. Thus saith the Lord of hosts, the God of Israel, 'Behold! I will bring evil upon this place, the which whosoever heareth, his ears shall tingle. Because they have forsaken me, and have estranged this place, and have burned incense in it unto other gods, whom neither they nor their fathers have known, nor the kings of Judah, and have filled this place with the blood of innocents; they have built also the high places of Baal, to burn their sons with fire for burnt-offerings unto Baal (which I commanded not, nor spake it, neither came it into my mind): *Therefore,* behold! the days come,' saith the Lord, 'that this place shall no more be called Tophet, nor the Valley of the sons of Hinnom, but the Valley of Slaughter; and I will make void the counsel of Judah and Jerusalem in this place, . . . and I will make this city desolate, and a hissing.'" Jer. xix. 3–8.

Such was the prevalence of open idolatry, and such its punishment, in the most spiritually-enlightened people upon the earth.

It is very true that the clearer light of Christianity has reduced the power of this gross form of falsehood, and yet human nature has unmistakably asserted its depravity in this direction even in the midst of the nominal Church of Christ. Before the fourth century after Christ was completed, images of our Saviour were introduced into the churches, and these paved the way for introducing images of the saints, so that, by the eighth century, the Christian churches were as full of statues as ever were the heathen temples; and before these marble saints the illiterate bowed in prayer and vow, and knew no other god but these. The object at first was, doubtless, to help the imagination to worship the true God through a visible symbol; and as Christ was God manifest in the flesh, it seemed perfectly proper to make a visible representation of Christ as a quickener of devotion. The very visibility and tangibility of the representation was a satisfaction to the worshiper; and this, together with the greater external ceremony that could be thrown around an image-worship, formed the bait to the gross idolatry of the mediæval Church and the Roman Church of to-day.

The all-wise and omniscient God knew man's frailty, and in this second commandment forbade the use in worship of any visible representation, even though it be of the divine Being himself in the person of Jesus Christ: "Thou shalt not make unto thee any likeness of anything *that is in heaven above;*" and the full expression of the context shows that the spiritual as well as the physical heaven is meant, the whole universe of God being included.

I need hardly stop to say that the use of two distinct sentences for one, where the latter qualifies the former, is a common Hebraism. We are not forbidden to *make* images, but to make them *in order to* bow down to them, or to bow down to them when made.

The only point at which this commandment touches us Protestant Christians is in our general tendency to rest in form rather than in spirit, and to place religion in the emotions rather than in the affections. This is a human frailty; and so long as we are human, we shall be open to the temptation. It has been suggested by prominent Protestants in this country that likenesses of distinguished Christian heroes should be placed in our churches, and we find everywhere in Europe that the Protestant churches are adorned with crucifixes, images of our Saviour on the cross, whose direct tendency is to beget an image-worship. Even the cross itself, if we use it in worship to bow down to it, is forbidden by this commandment; but the cross may be, and often *is*, used as a mere symbol of religious faith, where the crucifix would inevitably become an object of adoration.

The reason God gives for his command against idolatry needs our attention. It is that he is *a jealous God* (Él-kanna—θέος ζηλωτης). This expression is frequently used in the Old Testament, and in one place the

Lord declared to Moses that *his name is jealous.* The force of the phrase is perhaps best seen in the words of Moses to Israel when he gave them his parting advice, "for the Lord thy God is a consuming fire, even a jealous God" (Deut. iv. 24), a passage which is quoted and used by the apostle Paul in the Epistle to the Hebrews, where he is speaking of the future and eternal judgments of the Almighty. We must free the idea from the attachments which we give it from our view of *human* jealousy. There is no selfishness, no envy, no hatred, in God's jealousy. It is the abundant outflow of his holiness, which, by its own virtue, must either assimilate or destroy everything in the universe. It envelops in its grace, or it drives forth from its purity and from all the blessings which accompany its purity. When we say that God is a jealous God, we say that he is no passive Brahm, like the god of the Hindoos, but that he glows with zeal for all that is pure and good and holy and true, and is ever engaged actively in separating the holy and true from the unholy and false, striving to do it first by mercy, but if man makes that fail, then by the cutting off of his judgments. This character of God is especially alluded to in this second commandment, because this form of sin appeared the most seductive and the most obstinate. It were well, therefore, that God's character toward sin should here be especially exhibited.

The remainder of the commandment is really an enlargement on this character of holy jealousy, and the words startle us as we read them: "Visiting the iniquity of the fathers upon the children unto the third and fourth generation of them that hate me, and showing mercy unto thousands of them that love me and keep my commandments." "Is not this rank injustice, that children should be punished for their fathers' faults?" it is objected. "Am I to be sent to hell because my great-grandfather sinned?" It is very true that the human reason instinctively revolts at such a thought, and our unbiased instincts of the reason are generally correct. Our affections are depraved, warped and sinful, but our notion of right and wrong remains in its general force, even though we may be too ignorant to know all its detailed applications. It is at this very bar of our own judgment that we shall be condemned if we continue enemies to God. It is this comparatively healthful portion of our being, this which by its very nature cannot be essentially wicked or depraved, which exclaims against the punishment of children for parents' sins. And hence this portion of the second commandment is a stumbling-block to many. Besides the injustice of the thing, we see the fearful discouragement that it must generate in the soul against all attempts at return and reform. If I was condemned by my father's sin before I was born, why should I make any endeavor after anything good? It will be all a waste of time, a fostering, a delusion, an enlargement of disappointment. Now, all this exercise of mind in regard to God's description of himself would be avoided if we read the Bible more carefully and compared Scripture with Scripture. God expressly addresses those who thus entirely misconstrue his dealings and his character, and speaks thus by his prophet Ezekiel:

"What mean ye, that ye use this proverb concerning the land of Israel, saying, 'The fathers have eaten sour grapes and the children's teeth are set on edge?' . . . Behold, all souls are mine; as the soul of the father, so also the soul of the son is mine; *the soul that sinneth, it shall die.* . . . Yet say ye, Why? doeth not the son bear the iniquity of the father?" [misquoting this very commandment]. "When the son hath done that which is lawful and right, and hath kept all my statutes and hath done them, he shall surely live. The soul that sinneth, it shall die: the son shall *not* bear the iniquity of the father; . . . the righteousness of the righteous shall be upon him, and the wickedness of the wicked shall be upon him."

What could more fully show the exact justice of God and avert all objection to the misunderstood phrase in the second commandment? The key to the difficulty is in the words, "*of them that hate me,*" and the enunciation is just this—that where a man is opposed to God, rejecting his truth and salvation, he endorses and supports, and thus becomes responsible for, the guilt of his ancestors. The stream of guilt runs down from father to son with accumulating force till it ends in its appropriate judgment. This judgment, so far as it is spiritual and eternal, falls on each sinner in the line, but so far as it is earthly and temporal, it falls on him who brings the sinfulness to the top of the climax—who adds the last drop to the fullness of the cup. This is only true where the son or descendant is a hater of God.

Hence we see the meaning of such passages of revelation as these: in Job, where the patriarch speaks of the wicked, he says, "God layeth up his iniquity for his children." Isaiah says of Babylon: "Prepare slaughter for his children for the iniquity of their fathers," and again to the Jews: "I will recompense. . . your iniquities and the iniquities of your fathers together." So our Saviour, in pronouncing the fearful doom of the generation of ungodly and rebellious Jews among whom he lived, adds: "That upon you may come all the righteous blood shed upon the earth, from the blood of righteous Abel unto the blood of Zacharias son of Barachias, whom ye slew between the temple and the altar. Verily I say unto you, All these things shall come upon this generation."

This is the natural flow and consequence of sin, but grace can furnish a check, and roll back the tide, both in relation to the physical and spiritual results of iniquity. Hence, even of wicked Ahab, the willing instrument of his wife Jezebel's idolatries and cruelties, it is recorded, "And it came to pass, when Ahab heard these words [of the prophet Elijah], that he rent his clothes and put sackcloth upon his flesh and fasted and lay in sackcloth and went softly. And the word of the Lord came to Elijah, the Tishbite, saying, 'Seest thou how Ahab humbleth himself before me? Because he humbleth himself before me, I will not bring the evil in his days, but in his son's days will I bring the evil upon his house.'" So, also, the cry of the Psalmist is founded on this power of grace to check and cancel the issues of hereditary sin: "Oh remember not against us former iniquities," or, as the margin reads it, "Remember not against us the iniquities of them that were before us"—*i. e.*, our forefathers.

The subject is thus freed from all ideas

of injustice, for each one suffers for *his own sin*, made his own by appropriating it as an inheritance, and building on it, as on a foundation, his new sinfulness. Yet there is a mystery in this matter of the relation of paternity and sonship, in which we are simply to take God's word for it, recognize a corroborating analogy, and leave the rest for solution in a world of greater light and larger views. God's word shows clearly that there is a spiritual connection by blood descent. Every man begins where his father leaves off. If his father be evil, he starts with that amount of evil capital to use if he will, and if he be evil himself (as every man by nature is), then he actually uses that capital in his own practice of evil. If his father be good, then he starts with that amount of good capital to use if he will, though, on this side of the picture, every man's innate depravity modifies the correspondence. Hence men accumulate evil from generation to generation, but they do not accumulate good. All they can do is to check the evil, and hand down the example and precept for checking it to their posterity. It is for this reason, in this second commandment, we find that the *iniquity* of the fathers is visited upon the children, but the *good* of the fathers is not so visited.

The analogy to this fact of revelation we have in the matter of disease. Consumption, scrofula, and a thousand diseases, descend from parent to child. As these are purely physical, they do not involve necessarily the idea of punishment. They may be used by God as the richest blessings to the soul to all eternity, and we know that they are constantly so used. No man can call it an injustice, therefore, that he should have a diseased body because his father was a drunkard, because his diseased body is a *blessing*, if he only have a mind to make it so. God comes personally to every man (in his love for every creature he has made), and offers to make everything in him and around him to work together for his good. If man rejects this offer, and so lets his inherited disease be only a curse to him, let him not blame God for punishing the son for the father's sin. The son has *chosen* the punishment, of his free will. Even when, through grace, the infliction of the hereditary disease is made a blessing, there will be much temporary discomfort and pain; and so in the soul where sin is pardoned and the Spirit given, there will be habits and tendencies, much of the foul growth of hereditary sin, to cause temporary discomfort and pain. In neither case is it punishment, but affliction, which a parent can bring upon a child, even as you may bring affliction upon your neighbor by breaking his arm, he not at all consenting; and there is no more divine injustice in the one than in the other. Two thoughts naturally suggest themselves from this subject brought before us in the second commandment:

1st. *What a vast responsibility rests upon*

parents! The parent has it in his power to inflict life-long evil upon his child, and to increase the child's everlasting condemnation, unless the grace of God interfere. As a father by his debauched life, or even by a life simply careless of the laws of health, may entail disease upon his children—and he is just as responsible for injuring his children as if he had put the cup of poison to their lips—so a father may, by his disregard of the laws of God, entail spiritual disease and misery upon his children, and he is just as responsible for his children's ruin as was Satan responsible for Adam's fall.

Listen, then, ye that bend your souls to Mammon, thinking, dreaming, planning and wishing only about money, and ye that yield your talents and time to Fashion, feeding your poor starved souls on the frippery and flippancy of her fool's paradise—ye are not slaying yourselves, but your children, and preparing their hell of remorse! For your children's sake, if not for your own, stop, and seize the saving hand of Christ!

2d. *See the fullness of God's grace:* "And showing mercy unto thousands of them that love me and keep my commandments." Where the look of love and faith is put forth to Jesus, the whole condemnation, growing from ancestral sins, is stayed. And God is ever watching for the first acceptance of his proffered grace, that its victory may be made perfect. He will not, he *cannot*, compromise and compound with sin. It must go on in its lava torrent of corruption from generation to generation, sweeping everything before it into eternal despair, except the one divine rescue, not by compromise, but by substitution and atonement, be accepted. Wherever the soul takes Christ as its portion, God's holy jealousy burns no more against the sinner—the deliverance is immediate and complete. The love of Jesus is the pledge of the deliverance. Do I love to keep God's commandments? Then I love God; and if I love God, this is a clear sign that his Spirit is given me, and I am rescued from the long hereditary flood of guilt. *Out of Christ,* I was appropriating generations of iniquity and earning their doom. *In Christ,* I am appropriating his eternal life and glorious reward. The question to each of us is between *accumulated and accumulating guilt,* and *God's free, full grace in Christ.*

THE THIRD COMMANDMENT.

"*Thou shalt not take the name of the Lord thy God in vain: for the Lord will not hold him guiltless that taketh his name in vain.*"—EXODUS XX. 7.

THIS commandment holds its appropriate place in a regular gradation from the first. The first forbids the disregard of God in the heart, the second, such disregard in the outward act of worship, and this third (in its primary application), such disregard in the words of the mouth. God is to reign supreme in the heart, to be exclusive in his worship and to be mentioned always with reverence by the lips. The same holy jealousy which burns against the false worshiper for the same reason burns against the reckless speaker, where the subject of speech is the almighty and infinite Jehovah.

Where there is a want of reverence there is a want of allegiance. So far forth as a subject is disrespectful, he is rebellious; and all true government, especially the pure and holy government of God, must take cognizance of the rebellion in accordance with holiness and truth.

The illustration of this principle in the family is very apt. The boy who has learned to speak of his father with disrespect has learned to be disobedient, and so shows himself a violator of the root-law of family order and prosperity. Much of the filial ingratitude, undutiful neglect and rebellious independence of sons, over which so many fathers spend their vain sighs, would have been averted, if parents had recognized the two facts that implicit obedience is the absolute requisite of all true government, the keystone of moral order and strength, and that disobedience begins with the impudent and reckless word. The Christian parent should reverently imitate his heavenly Father, and not allow a single utterance of angry defiance or mocking jeer or careless disrespect from his child, but hold him guilty of a grievous sin.

With regard to this third commandment, the common view of its exclusive reference to vulgar profanity is entirely too contracted. That this low and vulgar sin is included in the prohibition is very evident; but were this its only meaning, the command would have no application to any one of respectable social standing. Simple refinement would raise a person above the infringement of this commandment. An examination of two expressions in the passage will open to us, I think, a wider horizon, and bring the commandment, in its personal and practical application, nearer home.

The first expression to which I refer is, "the name of the Lord thy God," or strictly, "the name of Jehovah thy God." The name of the Lord is not, on one hand, the mere articulate sound by which the mouth expresses the idea of Deity, nor is the phrase, on the other hand, a simple synonym for God. Scripture does not by this formula denote "the title of God," separating between God and his title, nor does it use a circumlocution and denote God himself, making "the Lord" and "the name of the Lord" equivalents, but it holds up God in his special character of *Jehovah, the covenant-making and covenant-keeping God of his own dear people.* "The name of Jehovah" means God, known and served under his revealed aspect of mercy, God appreciated as the pardoner of sin and giver of the spirit, the Jehovah or keeper of his precious promises to his people. For example, of the antediluvian piety it is said, "Then began men to call upon the name of the Lord"—*i. e.*, it was then that distinctive recognition was made of God's special provision of mercy for sinners. His name of Jehovah was received as indicating his relation to his believing people. A name is an expression of the personal substance, an exhibition of the essential character. God's name by which he delights to be known among men, is *Love*. He also says that his name is *Jealous*, but it is his name "Jehovah" which attaches him to his people, and which asserts his love and grace. His character of compassion is especially displayed in his word, and hence the Psalmist says, "Thou hast magnified thy word above all thy name"—that is, of all revelations of God's character, all expressions of his being, the written word is most full and complete. Here is the way of pardon and acceptance clearly portrayed.

Another conspicuous display of God's character, but only local and temporary in its personal contact, while universal in its possible application, is in the Lord Jesus Christ, and so Jesus is in a high sense "the name of Jehovah," and he calls himself this. You remember how, just before his last sufferings and death, he cried unto the

Father, "Father, glorify thy name," when he had said, just before, that it was himself, the Son of man, who should be glorified. Jesus was *the name of God*, or, as Paul declares, "the brightness of God's glory and the express image of his substance;" and we have no hesitation in seeing this bright glory of Jesus in the burning bush, the fiery cloudy pillar and all the theophanies of Old-Testament days. The frequent reference to the tabernacle or temple as the place which Jehovah had chosen *to put his name there*, asserts that the express image of Jehovah occupied that earthly habitation among his people. The name of Jehovah that was there placed was *the word of God*, who was in the beginning with God and who was God. The great Antitype was there present among his types. By the "*name* of Jehovah," then, we are to understand his manifestations to man, especially in his Scripture and in his Son, each of which is called, for a similar reason, "*the Word.*"

The second expression to which our attention should be directed is the phrase, "to take in vain." The literal rendering is, "thou shalt not lift up the name of Jehovah thy God lightly." Taking God's name in vain is not simply the using the divine name to support a falsehood, as some say who would make this commandment a prohibition of perjury, but it is also the use of that name in any cause or on any occasion where a due solemnity does not accompany the use. It is the flippant and thoughtless use of God's name. It is the taking up the name in the vacant, purposeless way in which we pluck off a leaf as we pass along the road—the use of the name, not only where the purpose is evil, but where there is no defined purpose at all. There need be no intention to mock or deride the holy name—and the thought of such mockery or derision may be quite abhorrent to the soul—yet there is a meddling with holy things by profane hands, and the careless perpetrator is therein a positive and active enemy to holiness and God. Again, there may be not only an absence of evil purpose, but, beyond an absence of all purpose, there may even be a purpose of good, but this purpose may be seized upon in so rash and ill-advised a way that the use of the divine name in it is a taking the name in vain, just as Uzzah's touching the ark of God, even to stay it upon the cart and prevent its fall, was a sin of profanity, and called for the divine punishment.

From these thoughts upon the two principal phrases in the third commandment, we are prepared to see its true scope, as bearing upon all use other than a *devout* and *reverential* use of all that expresses God's character and being, whether it be his verbal name, his written word, his only-begotten Son who has declared him, or any of the great truths which are brought to the heart and conscience by the Holy Spirit. Let us look a moment at each of these divisions of thought, and apply a faithful examination to our own souls.

1. In respect to *God's verbal name*, we are not to be satisfied with our freedom from the coarse profanity which culture and good-breeding forbid, but we are to remove the habit of using the holy name in ordinary conversation in which the use has no religious character. We are not to call a wretched and forlorn person or thing "God-forsaken," or to hail a gift as a "God-send," when, in using these epithets, we have no design to use their full meaning, and therefore have not the proper attitude of mind for their utterance. The use is both an insult to God and a debauchery to the soul.

2. In respect to *God's written word*, we are to take it up with reverence both in our hearts and on our tongues. Any other action toward the holy Bible is taking God's name in vain. A just view of this forbids our travesties of Scripture, or the burlesque use of language indissolubly associated with

Scripture in our minds, all witticisms, by pun or conundrum, in relation to the sacred words of revelation, in short, anything which to our sinful natures would tend to debase or vulgarize the heavenly truths of the Bible through the laws of association. It also forbids all *mere* use of Scripture for its story and history, for its geography and science, for its language and literature. The use of its letter without its spirit is a dishonor to God. The only way in which this exhibition of God is to be rightly used is in finding God therein. For that purpose he gave it, and a rejection of that use is an assertion of self before God. The Bible is given to show sinners the way of salvation and holiness, and, as before said, any other ultimate use of the divine Book is the taking God's name in vain.

But 3, and chiefly, in relation to *Jesus and the great, eternal truths* which the Holy Spirit introduces to the soul. To each man comes through his conscience a summons from God to give heed to his future spiritual and eternal condition. A sense of sin, and of unrest by reason of sin, oppresses every child of Adam, and God is known, even to the untutored soul, as a God of justice. His name of "Jealous" is daily seen and understood by the most ignorant and worldly, and it is to all such that he comes to reveal himself as "Love." He comes, in Jesus and his blood, to seek and save the lost. Christ, with his saving truth, is that name of Jehovah which was proclaimed to Moses in the cleft of Sinai's rock, and which is now proclaimed, through Church and Christian and Bible, to every soul.

"*Jehovah, Jehovah God, merciful and gracious, long-suffering and abundant in goodness and truth, keeping mercy for thousands, forgiving iniquity and transgression and sin, and that will by no means clear the guilty; visiting the iniquity of the fathers upon the children, and upon the children's children, unto the third and to the fourth generation.*"

This is the manifestation of Jesus, the Saviour, who saves, but not at the expense of justice, who saves without a compromise with iniquity, who lets sin wreak its fierce wrath, either on himself (and there is the sinner's salvation) or on the sinner (and there is the sinner's damnation), with the sinner's choice to decide which it shall be. This knowledge of God's active grace in Jesus is the possession of you who read these pages. "This is the true Light which lighteth every man that cometh into the world." This wonderful Jesus with his glorious truth is the *name of God* entrusted to your keeping. You have taken it up into your cognition and thought. *How* have you taken it up? With admiration and gratitude and devotion? Have you used it as a treasure from heaven, cherishing it in your bosom, and ready to part with all else rather than part with *it?*

Have you loved to learn more and more of God through his disclosed name, seeing the Father in Jesus, and studying intently and delightedly the divine glory that shines forth from the Son? Have you felt that life's sunshine was in the smile of Christ, from whose gospel sprang all true halcyon days? Have these been your experiences before the glad tidings? Or have you met them with an averted front? Have you taken up this great name of Jehovah in vain? Have you treated the message from heaven like a song to be forgotten? Have you let it rest upon your ears and forbidden it your heart, putting it in company with theories and fantasies, as of like weight and worthy of equal regard?

I do not ask you, Have you derided the gospel and its Author?—*that* you would be far from doing—but, Have you *neglected* the gospel—played with it, as a man may play with a glove while he is talking to a friend —used its priceless truths without attention and so without respect? If this is your record, be assured that God does not hold you guiltless. Such a precious treasure in your hand must be either a great blessing or a great curse to you. As a man is gifted from God, the possible extremes of his destiny widen. A brighter heaven and a darker hell unfold with every new boon. This gospel in your possession is a mighty responsibility; and if you slight it, you are taking God's name in vain, and choosing the penalty rather than the reward. God gave you the gospel for a purpose—the purpose of glorifying him and glorifying your own soul; you take it for another purpose or for no purpose. Can you have any doubt as to what the end of this opposition will be?

There is a parallel thought for the Christian who neglects the glorious name of Jehovah, the Christian who allows the gay and foolish world to wheedle him into its arms, who sinks down into a semi-legalism, where duty is all hard work and the liberty of God's children appears very much like bondage. This Christian is really trifling with the gospel—he is taking God's name in vain. He has seen the grace of God in Christ and acknowledged it by faith, and now that eternal gospel, on whose perpetual flow depends his life, is slighted for the tinseled and bedizened rivals of an hour. The due and proper reverence of God's name implies a very honest and a very hearty searching of the Scriptures, it implies a sincere and ready use of prayer, and it implies a devotion of *time*, TIME, TIME, to the contemplation and worship of the Redeemer; and unless a Christian exhibits this style of piety, he is breaking the third commandment as truly as yon rough blasphemer in the street, at whose profanity he shrinks back in horror and disgust. The sin of each, when analyzed, is a disregard of the sanctity of God's manifestations and of their requirements, a worldly and profane posture of the soul toward the reachings forth of God's grace; and they only differ in this, that the one shows his neglect less openly to others, by negative rather than positive signs, while the other hangs out his flag, and with his words exposes the carelessness of his heart.

It is a most solemn thought to us that the infinite God, the blessed and only Potentate, the King of kings and Lord of lords, who only hath immortality, dwelling in the light which no man can approach unto, whom no man hath seen nor can see, to whom belong honor and power everlasting, brings his name to us as a treasure and confides it to our care, saying, "Occupy till I come." The history of our eternity will begin with our use or abuse of this keepsake. Its injury or neglect will tell fearfully against us in that day when our relation to this name will be seen to be the criterion of our salvation. Then will this Name (as including every expression and manifestation of God) be recognized both by exultant and despondent souls as "the brightness of his glory and the express image of his person," centering in the Lord Jesus Christ, whose holy rays must ever illuminate or ever consume. In this view, how vast is the import of the third commandment! Not one of us can remain unconcerned before the voice which rolls through the ages from Sinai, and breaks to-day upon our ears, "Thou shalt not take the name of the Lord thy God in vain, for the Lord will not hold him guiltless that taketh his name in vain."

The Fourth Commandment.

"*Remember the Sabbath-day to keep it holy. Six days shalt thou labor and do all thy work, but the seventh day is the Sabbath of the Lord thy God: in it thou shalt not do any work, thou, nor thy son, nor thy daughter, thy man-servant, nor thy maid-servant, nor thy cattle, nor thy stranger that is within thy gates: for in six days the Lord made heaven and earth, the sea, and all that in them is, and rested the seventh day: wherefore the Lord blessed the Sabbath day and hallowed it.*"—Exodus xx. 8–11.

THIS commandment holds a remarkable position in the Decalogue. It lies between those which touch our duty to God and those which touch our duty to man. Before it are the three commandments which enjoin reverence for Jehovah in his essence and expression (an avoidance of a wrong expression, and the proper regard for the true), and after it are the six commandments which enjoin respect for the rights and welfare of our fellow-men. Between these two distinct departments of the Decalogue is found this commandment regarding the Sabbath—not a few parenthetic words, but the longest and most minute of all the commandments.

The Sabbath is said to be the day of *Jehovah*—it is "the Sabbath of the Lord thy God"—and hence its law appropriately adjoins those which expose our duty to God; but our Saviour also tells us that the Sabbath was made for *man*, and hence the Sabbath ordinance appropriately adjoins those which expose our duty to man. It belongs to both branches of the Decalogue. Its position tells us that a breach of the Sabbath is a direct insult to God, and is also a direct injury to man, weakening the power of a day which is eminently a blessing to the human race.

This remarkable position of the Sabbath commandment is proof incontrovertible of its binding character for all men in all time.

We have on a former occasion seen that the Decalogue has this universal application—that it was intended for no circumscribed period or locality; and here we find in that Decalogue—nay, in its very heart, occupying one-third of its bulk and most intimately interwoven with its texture—the divine order to sanctify the Sabbath-day. This is enough to satisfy any candid mind. We need not go farther and show that the Sabbath was expressly recognized by Israel before the Decalogue was given, at the time when the manna was first sent, and when on the sixth day the people collected sufficient food for two days that they might not profane the Sabbath, where the narrative shows that it was a deep-rooted religious observance. We need not refer to the division of time into the unnatural portions of seven days, as seen in the history of the world from the time of Noah to that of Moses, which so clearly proves the existence of a Sabbath before the people of

Israel had a being even in the person of their father and founder Abraham. It is sufficient to show the command of the Sabbath engraven by the finger of God most conspicuously among the ten items of his great moral law, and placed in awful concealment within the holy ark as indicative of its peculiar sanctity,—I say, it is sufficient to see it in this company and these circumstances to be assured of its important relation to every subject of the divine government.

There are two expressions in the command itself which testify to this universality of application.

1. "*Remember* the Sabbath-day." It is no new institution which you are now to learn about for the first, but it is an old observance, not Israelitish, but human, Noachic and Adamic, which you, God's Israel, are to *remember*, that you may sustain it in its purity, just as you are to sustain a true and spiritual worship as against idolatry. This

is the purport of the phrase. Israel was selected and made the people of God by his grace, that in them, as in an ark, might be deposited and preserved the truths, moral and practical, which God had given the race. The chief advantage of Israel was that to them were committed the oracles of God. These oracles were not made for Israel, but Israel, as such, was made for them. In this ark—this early church—were preserved and concealed, by reason of man's depravity, the truths which would have been altogether corrupted and dissipated if left to man's ordinary care. This accounts for the word "remember"—"*remember* the Sabbath-day."

2. The other expression which proves the universality of its application (in addition to its very position in the Decalogue) is the reason given for the divine order—"because in six days Jehovah made heaven and earth, the sea and all that in them is, and rested the seventh day: *wherefore* Jehovah blessed

the Sabbath-day and hallowed it." The reason began at the creation, and therefore the observance began at the creation. Adam and Eve in Paradise kept the Sabbath-day; for the reason for its observance, as here given in the law, was as cogent with *them* as it was with *Israel* at Sinai, or as it is with *us* to-day.

I refer to this perpetual obligation of the Sabbath, because a flippant criticism and a naturalistic and rationalistic theology are endeavoring to persuade the Christian world that everything that was found in Israel was a mark of bondage from which we are happily free—an error which has just this ground of truth, that from the *ceremonies* of Israel we are expressly freed; but the Sabbath was never an appurtenance of the Jewish ceremonial, any more than the worship of one God was, but both were requirements of God upon the race, and of course especially urged upon the Jews as representatives of the true religion. The

Jews, as a *typical* Church, had much that was to be abrogated when the antitype should come; but as a *Church*, they had much that was to remain wherever and whenever the true Church of God was. The position of the Sabbath in the Decalogue shows us to which of these two classes it belongs.

The question in regard to *the seventh and the first days* of the week, as to which is the true Sabbath, is one entirely apart from the question of Sabbath observance. A doubt as to the proper day cannot alter a conviction of the general duty of keeping a Sabbath. The Jew and the Seventh-day Baptist, if sincere, are equally Sabbath observers with others who keep the first day of the week. We all agree in the duty, although we differ on the minor point of the day. Our own observance of the first day is in accordance with the uniform usages of the apostles and of the apostolic Church, the day in which Jehovah-Jesus rested from his work of the new creation being substituted for the day in which he rested from his work of the old creation. A change of day very appropriately marked a change of dispensation, while the observance of a Sabbath in each marked the oneness of the two dispensations in their essential character.

Leaving these questions, we proceed to consider the two chief thoughts in connection with the command—first, What is the idea of the Sabbath? and, secondly, What is its proper observance?

I. *What is the idea of the Sabbath?* It had its origin in God's *resting* on that day. Of course, this is an anthropomorphism. God is said to work and to rest, and the figure of a man working and resting is placed before our minds. The figure would not be given us unless there were in it the nearest approach to the incomprehensible truth itself. It *is* true, though not the *whole* truth, and we can rest safely in it until we know God more fully. There was an actual rest with God on the seventh day, whether that day was twenty-four hours or twenty-four thousand years long. The commandment further orders man to labor six days, and to do no work on the Sabbath. And *again*, the word "Sabbath" means "rest." Most certainly, then, the great idea of the Sabbath is the idea of rest. This the apostle clearly indicates in his argument in the fourth chapter of his Epistle to the Hebrews, where he shows us that the Sabbath was a type of the great Sabbath-rest of heaven in store for the saints of God; for, he says, just as God rested from working on the seventh day, so the saints of God will rest from toil when they reach that Sabbatism.

On this passage Moses Stuart remarks: "As God ceased from his work on the seventh day, and enjoyed holy delight in the contemplation of what he had done, so the believer, in a future world, will cease from all his toils and sufferings here and look back with holy delight on the struggles through which he has passed, and the labors which he has performed for the sake of the Christian cause."

This idea of rest, involved *in*, and denoted *by*, the Sabbath, was further shown in the institution of *the sabbatical year*, which was a local and temporary ordinance among the Israelites. Its institution occurs in the midst of other civil and ceremonial laws given at Mount Sinai, and runs thus: "When ye come into the land which I give you, then shall the land keep a Sabbath unto the Lord. Six years thou shalt sow thy field, and six years thou shalt prune thy vineyard and gather in the fruit thereof; but in the seventh year shall be a *Sabbath of rest* unto the land: thou shalt neither sow thy field nor prune thy vineyard. That which groweth of its own accord of thy harvest thou shalt not reap, neither gather the grapes of thy vine undressed, for it is a *year of rest* unto the land." Then it is beautifully added, "And the Sabbath of the land shall be meat for you." It is as if God said, "Do not grudge this loss of corn and wine, but remember in your self-denial, as regards *them*, that your spiritual nourishment is augmented by the year of rest, in the trial of your faith and in its typical instruction so vividly brought before your souls."

In the realization of a sabbatical rest we see a marked contrast with the time immediately preceding. There have been six days of active labor, and straightway the quiet of the Sabbath supervenes. There have been six busy years of sowing and reaping, and then follows without any gradual preparation the sabbatic year of agricultural repose. The transition is *abrupt*, and so most marked. Again, we note that the observance of the rest is *unnatural*. Man would not stop his work on the seventh day, nor would an Israelite have stayed his sowing and reaping in the seventh year except by direct command of God. On the contrary, it would appear to the natural man a waste of time and opportunity in either case. Hence the observance of a Sabbath is an act of faith—a faith which *abruptly* ceases from a natural sequence and makes an unnatural hiatus. It is true that physiologists have discovered that the Sabbath is most beneficent in its influences on health and physical life, but this is a discovery made by Christian investigation, and not a natural motive for Sabbath-keeping. It is a token of the goodness and wisdom of God, who mingles our spiritual and temporal good in the same institution, but to man subjectively it would never be a practical argument for an exact seventh-day rest.

Having thus seen that the idea of the Sabbath is that of a *rest seized and entered upon by faith*, we are prepared to take up the last and most important inquiry—

II. *What is its proper observance?* My first remark is this, that *the Jewish civil and ceremonial law can give us no hint as to its proper observance.* A man found gathering sticks upon the Sabbath-day was put to death by stoning while Israel was still in the wilderness. This execution was in accordance with the civil laws of the Jews in regard to the observance of the Sabbath: "Ye shall kindle no fire throughout your habitations upon the Sabbath-day." This was the express order of the civil law. The man was gathering sticks for a fire, and thus *virtually* kindling a fire and breaking the civil law, the penalty for which was death. This detailed form of Sabbath-keeping is no more binding on us in the present dispensation than is the command to abstain from the wearing of linsey-woolsey. Lev. xix. 19.* All these *specific* commands formed parts of that great typical teaching

* "Neither shall a garment mingled of linen and woolen come upon thee."

which ended in our Saviour's advent. They then, by reason of the substance taking the place of the shadow, became, so far as the observance and use went, *στοιχεία*, "elements" or "rudiments of the world," "weak and beggarly"—that is, very inefficient expositions of truth compared with the full gospel of Jesus. They thenceforward became *illustrations*, and lost their former province as first principles and *guides* of truth. We are, therefore, to mark the clear distinction of the *general* ordinance of the Sabbath, which was *universal*, for all men in all time and all lands, and *the specific laws* of the Sabbath, which were *particular* for Israelites in the time of their polity and the land of Canaan only. It is with such an understanding that we can rightly say that the Christian Sabbath is not the Jewish Sabbath. The mistake of the Puritan Sabbath is in a lack of regard for this distinction, as if the internal police of the Jewish people before Sinai and in Palestine was to be copied by Anglo-Saxons in Massachusetts and Connecticut. Again and again the apostles declare that the Christian Church is released from the bondage of the burdensome "touch not, taste not, handle not" ordinances, and that Christians are brought directly in contact with the great spiritual truths which these ordinances adumbrated. But they add that we must not use our liberty from these detailed outward observances as an occasion for the flesh—that is, as an opportunity for our worldliness to have vent and spread itself.

This leads me to my second remark, that *the European Sabbath is a false Sabbath.* In leaping forth from the strict externals of the Jewish Sabbath, Christians (so-called) in continental Europe have made the Sabbath a mere holiday, a day of gayety and light amusement; in which, it is true, they abstain from their wonted labor in craft and trade, but utterly forgetting that the Sabbath rest is a *sacred* rest—that not only are we to do no work, but also to keep the day HOLY. The Puritans ran into legalism, and these European Christians into license. They both have failed to understand the true spiritual character of the Sabbath. In opposition to both these extremes, we remark that *the Sabbath is God's day.* He has given it his own holy name. "The Sabbath of the Lord thy God," he calls it in his commandment to the human race, spoken from Sinai, and the Holy Spirit calls it "*the Lord's day,*" in the New Testament. This fact shows us that its rightful observance must have regard to our right relation to God. The soul must be turned Godward. Worship becomes most appropriate, and with it the study of God's character and will as given us in the gospel of Jesus Christ. No Sabbath-keeping is a right observance that does not thus recognize the day as *God's* day, that does not bring the soul into the positive and active contemplation of God and his word. It is in this, and in this only, that the day is made *holy*.

Let no one here suggest as an objection that the holiness of the Sabbath was a mere *ceremonial* holiness, a mere external distinction. This is not so. When God uttered the order for the Sabbath from Sinai, there WAS *no ceremonial* in Israel, and hence *no ceremonial holiness*. The word "holy" has its full original force—it refers to the heart of man and its humble recognition and acceptance of the divine; and the keeping of the Sabbath holy can mean nothing else, Godward, but a fervent religious regard of its hours as given to draw the soul nearer to God.

Here, again, notice that while the Sabbath is God's day, *it is also "made for man"*—not for man's frivolity and worldly indulgence, any more than for man's free run in sin, but for man *as man*, as the image of God, as he was made and intended to be by his Creator. "The Sabbath was made for man," cries the licentious heart that keeps the Sabbath by breaking it. He forgets that he has lost his manhood and become a fool and a beast, and the Sabbath was not made for a fool or a beast, but for *man*. It was made to improve and exalt man, to further his highest interests, to foster in him the work of God's Spirit, to *unworld* him and *inheaven* him, and to do all this by giving his *time*, *precious time*, to abstract his attention from the cares and occupations of the ordinary life, and to fasten it upon the infinite interests of the spiritual and eternal life. If the Sabbath was given for anything lower than this, if it was given for the benefit of man's body or present life, why is it found amid the loftiest thoughts of God and the profound commands that search out man's heart and speak to his entire immorality? Away with such trifling before the glorious words of Jehovah!

We see, then, from the two considera

tions, that the Sabbath is God's day and that it is made for man, that it is to be by man *spiritually observed for his spiritual good.* This conclusion, carefully noted, does away with all riding, sailing, visiting, promenading, gaming,—in short, with all indulgence in mere amusements, however innocent in themselves and proper on other days; and, on the other hand, it does away with all mere ritualism and formality, with all mere external strictness, and, indeed, with *all strictness that is not properly and legitimately connected with spiritual growth.* A forced asceticism is as repugnant to the truth as is a wild license—they are two forms of the same self-righteousness. The only external duty clearly commanded by God in the universal commandment of the Sabbath is abstinence from our usual occupations. Our labor and work are to be done in the six days, and abruptly given up on the Sabbath. *That* much was an absolute necessity to a true Sabbath-keeping, but, *beyond* that, the Bible, our only guide, tells us nothing. It shows us, indeed, that Christians were accustomed to assemble upon the Christian Sabbath, which is a most natural prompting of the renewed heart. What more natural to such, upon a day wherein worldly work is omitted for spiritual purposes, than to come together in search for the spiritual gain? This coming together may take any form—it may be a prayer-meeting, a conference-meeting, a Bible-meeting, an experience-meeting, or all combined,—there may be only one in the day or a dozen. In this there is the largest liberty. We must rid ourselves of the false notion that two stately meetings in a pulpited and pewed church are the true *qualem* and *quantum* of Sabbath duties, even so far as public meetings go. Often one warm prayer-meeting is worth them both. Bring Christians together with Bible, prayer and song, and you have a true meeting of the Church, complete in every part. Anything more than that is adventitious. There is a general rule, however, for God's people, which the Holy Spirit gives us, which we must apply to the Sabbath as to everything else —it is that everything be done decently and in order. There should be no unbecoming looseness and irregularity in outward observances; that would be occasion of scoffing to the world, and an obstacle to our own true progress, as it would tempt us to frequent omissions and neglect, and all indifference toward public worship is a mark of low spirituality. Let a proper uniformity in our methods be observed, and let no rash and rude changes be made. Let the duties which we owe to the Church be fully and gladly performed. In this, as in everything, let not our liberty, our undoubted liberty, to choose our own way of keeping the Sabbath holy according to our conscience—I say, let not this liberty prove with any of us an occasion for the flesh.

While we take this position from God's word on the *positive* side, we can on the *negative* side as certainly warn every one against allowing the business of the week to encroach on the time and thoughts of the Sabbath.

Christian merchant, do you make up your accounts on the Sabbath? Christian lawyer, do you study your case on the Sabbath? Christian woman, do you carry on your housekeeping or social employments upon the Sabbath? Christian youth, do you prepare your school-tasks upon the Sabbath? If so, you are laboring and doing all your work on seven days, and not six, and you are not keeping the Sabbath holy. The first necessity of the Sabbath—that is, your time and mind being free to study God and his word—this first necessity of the Sabbath you despise. You might as well take a shop upon the public thoroughfare, and keep it wide open for customers upon the Sabbath; *that* would not be a whit worse treatment of God's command. Why have you not faith in the God of the Sabbath, that he will guard your interests, and not let you suffer from the observance of his day, as he guarded Israel, and provided for the support of a whole nation while the whole land kept a Sabbath-year? Your want of faith makes you a Sabbath-breaker, and your Sabbath-breaking is constantly weakening your faith.

The only occasions in which God permits his command to receive an apparent disobedience is when an absolute necessity or a pious activity makes the exception. The priests in the temple profaned the Sabbath. They were obliged, by the necessities of the law of God, to remove and change the show-bread, to snuff the candles and to perform the other service of the temple on the Sabbath-day. Our Lord taught that it was right to heal disease or relieve any case from pressing distress on the Sabbath. These exceptions are very easily discriminated. Does the question of traveling on the Sabbath arise? or of using the street-car, or a hired carriage? Let it be answered by no categoric universal "It is right," or "It is wrong," but let it be answered by each person on each occasion, "Does my piety prompt this? or am I seeking my own pleasure and amusement?" If I am in a street-car upon the Sabbath, on an errand of piety, it is as well as if I were on my feet or in my bed. I am *right*, while another at my side, who is taking his ride for pleasure on his way to dine with a friend or on his way to the Central Park, is as certainly *wrong*. If everybody would act in regard to the Sabbath from this standpoint of personal piety, we should find no difficulty in practice. Let the directors of the public conveyances observe the same rule, and decide as to running their vehicles on the Sabbath, by the consideration, not what is gainful, but what is godly, and their decisions will be blessed of God. Each soul must be its own judge. My use of a public conveyance upon the Sabbath does *not* justify or endorse the action of the directors in running it, nor does their action in running it justify or endorse my use of it. Each case is wholly independent of the other, and is to be judged by its motive. I cannot throw my sin on the directors, and they cannot throw their sin on me; neither can my pious action benefit them, nor their pious action benefit me.

The outer law of the Sabbath to the Christian is simply to abstain from the ordinary daily labor; the inner law of the Sabbath is to keep it holy. Like all the other commandments, it is solely and intensely personal, and its keeping and breaking can only be known to one's own soul and to God, who seeth the heart. It has an external and visible part, as have the convocation of saints, and baptism, and the Lord's Supper, and the reading of the Word, but it also has its internal and invisible part, which is its heart and marrow, and here the right observance of the Sabbath must begin. Let us, then, give the Sabbath its full value to our souls by the especial and assiduous cultivation of our spiritual knowledge and affections on the holy day. Let us spend much of it in prayer and private meditation, in close and happy communion with Jesus, and the rest of it (in company with the same Jesus) in conversing with and teaching others of God's love in Christ. If we are careful and watchful here, I doubt not we shall make no mistake in the outward observance of the day.

The common fault of Christians consists in letting the world lead, instead of leading the world. In nothing, perhaps, is this seen so much as in topics of conversation. We let our worldly friends control the discourse, taking their subjects from the business or the trifles of daily life, while we have a perfect right to introduce a religious theme, and yet keep silent through fear. Especially on the Sabbath let our boldness be seen, and as we mingle with worldly friends let them see that we have higher matters to talk of than any they can bring. With all courtesy and with all modesty, yet with all frankness, let us speak earnestly and gratefully of Jesus, his gospel and his salvation. There is no need of a sombre face or of deep-drawn sighs. We ought to have a cheerful face and a merry heart, showing our sympathy with everybody and our pleasure in their welfare. Let us always make the Sabbath a *cheerful* day, *as Phariseeism does not,* and let us always make it a *holy* day, *as worldliness does not.*

Its observance is an injunction, most precise and most solemn, of our God. Obedience will enrich us with unspeakable blessings, and disobedience will entail upon us grievous woes. We cannot break the Sabbath with impunity. Let us away with a conceited philosophy, and bow humbly before the law. It has its motive in God's infinite wisdom and love, and its mighty results will be developed in the glorious future before every eye, and will vindicate its divine Author. Then shall we be able to judge of the length and breadth of its worth and of the divine favor in its gift, when we shall stand purified and glorified with the purity and glory of our Redeemer, in the midst of the heavenly Sabbatism.

Until then, let us all faithfully "remember the Sabbath-day to keep it holy."

THE FIFTH COMMANDMENT.

"*Honor thy father and thy mother, that thy days may be long upon the land which the Lord thy God giveth thee.*"—EXODUS xx. 12.

THE two tables of the law are usually held to have been written respectively with regard to our duties to God and our duties to man. And the second table of the law is generally supposed to have begun with this commandment. But if there was an equal amount of writing on each table, the commandment of the Sabbath would be two-sevenths on the first tablet and five-sevenths on the second tablet—a fact which would harmonize with the view we have taken of the double character of the fourth commandment, as including both our duty to God and our duty to man, and as exhibiting the Sabbath both as the Lord's day and the day for man. In either case, however, this commandment to honor father and mother is the first which looks entirely to a relative human duty. It is conspicuous among the commandments of the second table for another reason. It is the only one of these six which is not negatively expressed. The others read, "*Thou shalt not* do this or that," but this is positive: "*Honor* thy father and thy mother." There is yet another fact which makes it peculiarly prominent among these six commandments. It has a special promise of reward to its observers, to which the apostle refers in these words: "Honor thy father and thy mother, *which is the first commandment with promise*, that it may be well with thee and thou mayest live long on the earth."

Now, why is this command so conspicuous among the commandments of the law? Why does it stand before and above the command regarding the fearful crime of murder, bearing these three tokens of its superiority? I can only account for it by seeing in the parental relation the type of God's relation to us, and hence in the duties of children a type of our duties to God. I see that obedience is the foundation of all effective and righteous government, involving respect and homage toward authority, and so producing and maintaining harmony in the whole; and I see that this obedience is especially inculcated in the family, because in the highest typical sense the parent is as God to the children. There is thus a close alliance of this command with those of the first table, and hence we see it (in Leviticus) especially coupled with the sabbatical commandment: "Ye shall fear every man his mother and his father, and keep my Sabbaths: I am Jehovah your God." Lev. xix. 3.

Let us, in meditating upon the command, regard, *first*, the promise annexed, and then, *secondly*, the nature of the duty enjoined.

I. *The Promise.*—"That thy days may be long upon the land which the Lord thy God giveth thee."

In the rehearsal of the Decalogue by Moses, given in Deuteronomy v. 16, we find the promise expanded. This commandment, as there given, has the additional words, "as the Lord thy God hath commanded thee," and also, "and that it may go well with thee." So that the two together read thus, "Honor thy father and thy mother, as the Lord thy God hath commanded thee, that thy days may be prolonged, and that it may go well with thee, in the land which the Lord thy God giveth thee." The former of these two phrases adds to the solemnity and emphasis of the commandment, the latter to the point and power of the promise. It is as if God said, "Honor thy father and thy mother—this is no human expedient, but a divine order, founded in eternal truth; and in the obedience of this command thou shalt prolong thy life, not in wretchedness and evil, but in a true and continual prosperity."

The promise is of a long and prosperous life. It is so plain that it can admit of no other interpretation. The only question can be, "Is it an *individual* or a *national* life that is here meant?" But this is answered, *first*, by noticing that the command can only be kept by an individual person, and by a nation only as a number of individuals; and hence, as the command is only addressed to the individual, the prolongation of the individual life must be intended. The "thy" of "*thy* days" must refer to the same person as the "thy" of "*thy* father and *thy* mother." It is answered, *secondly*, that a long national career of prosperity presupposes and implies a goodly degree of personal longevity and prosperity, and that the latter is a cause of the former, while the former could in no sense be considered a cause of the latter. From these considerations, we hold that the promise of long life is directly and primarily to the individual who is obedient to this command, and then indirectly and secondarily to the nation of which he is a part. One man obeying this command will prolong a prosperous life, but one man only would not prolong the nation's prosperous life if all the rest of the people were riotous and disorderly. If, however, the bulk of the people should observe this command, then the whole national life would be preserved in prosperity. This is clearly the declaration of the promise—a promise which, like the command, belongs, not to Israel, but to the whole world. The man who honors his father and mother shall have a long and prosperous career; the nation which shows honor to its fathers and mothers, the nation wherein this filial respect is the general habit, shall have a long and prosperous career. We find, historically, that the Jews were accustomed to cover their disrespect for parents by the trick of "Corban;" and this fact reveals one of the secrets of their downfall.

What the connection is between filial piety and a long life, other than the connection of God's sovereign pleasure, it is not for us to say. We are not of those who feel that a *natural* cause must be found for every sequence in God's dealings, least of all, that it must be a natural cause within our limited knowledge of natural causes. It becomes us to be more childlike before God's words, to take their plain meaning, and not to wrest them in order to bring them within the reach of our petty philosophy. There is a large amount of practical infidelity which would take everything that God says and sift it through its own rationalistic sieve, and boldly reject whatever will not pass through. It is this which would explain away the promise of the text by saying that, *as a general thing*, if a child obey his parents, he will be kept from danger by thus using their prudence and experience, and that the commandment has this general statement of a probable long life to a child from this natural cause. The prosperity, likewise, would be a prosperity which would *naturally* grow out of harmony between child and parent arising from the child's obedience, wherein the parent would do everything to further the child's interests.

Now, in answer to such a view, let us note that this is no philosophical statement made by man, but *a promise made by God.* It is true as God is true, *not proximately true,* as are man's apophthegms. It can have no real exception, any more than the "Come unto me, and I will give you rest," or the "Believe on the Lord Jesus Christ, and thou shalt be saved," can have exceptions. The man who keeps this commandment is full possessor of the promise, or else the promise is a delusion.

But the objector cries, "Do you mean to

say that every one who has died young has been disobedient to his parents, for every one who had honored them would have lived to old age?" We reply that there is *one apparent exception*—where the soul itself prefers to leave this world for a better, and where, therefore, the letter of the promise yields to its spirit, and God, instead of continuing the saint upon earth, takes him to his desired home in heaven. Where this exception does not occur, we must believe that every one who dies before old age has disregarded this command. Very holy people are found to be defective in some direction. We can recall some sincerely pious persons who had very violent tempers, some who were very indolent, some who were very forgetful of others' interests. They would, at times, grieve over these errors, and perhaps gain strength against them, but *there*, nevertheless, the black spots on their character were visible. So we have seen saints who were forward in every good work, walking, like Zachariah and Elizabeth, in all the commandments of God blameless, patterns of holiness to the Church, and yet who had not faith to believe that God would be a God of salvation to their children, and so their children went astray like the wild ass' colts. These are the eccentricities, the mysterious freaks of piety, hard to account for, but that cannot be denied as existing, by any Christian observer. In like manner, we may find excellent people, hearts that love Jesus and receive his blood of atonement, who, most inconsistently, are deficient in respect to their filial duties of reverence and regard.

But the objector says again, "How can long life be a blessing to the Christian? Is not translation to heaven his desideratum?" The answer is, *first*, that God would not have promised long life so often to man as a reward if it were not a veritable blessing. He remembers that we are dust, he knows that we are weak, he makes allowance for our low degree of faith and aspiration, he stoops to our level in his promise, and so promises us long life as a prize for faithful conduct in a certain direction. *Secondly*, this does not interfere with the higher desire of a Paul to depart and be with Christ, which is far better.

I have seen the saints of the Lord who in the very spring-time of youth plumed their wings for their heavenly flight, who longed to soar away, and to whom the fairest attractions, and the purest, on earth were of no effect to withdraw their eager eyes from celestial prospects. By their own consent and desire, God could waive the fulfillment of this promise of long life because its very meaning was null in their case. But these cases are rare. To most Christians a long life on earth is, as it was to Hezekiah (good man that he was), a desirable boon, and God regards their feelings and considers it so, and therefore promises it on certain conditions, one of which is respect to parents. "My son, forget not my law, but let thy heart keep my commandments, for length of days and long life and peace shall they add to thee." Prov. iii. 1, 2. "Honor thy father and thy mother, that thy days may be long in the land which the Lord thy God giveth thee." The only other condition to which this promise is annexed is that of "dwelling in the secret place of the Most High" (Ps. xci.), in regard to which, of the man who *habitually* lives in the fear and faith of God, it is said by Jehovah, "With long life will I satisfy him."

Thus much, then, for the promise. Let us now consider—

II. *The nature of the duty enjoined:* "Honor thy father and thy mother." The word "*cabbed*" is very strong; it strictly means "load with honor," and is often used in reference to the Deity. Obedience is only one of the more prominent practical forms of this honor. The honor strikes deeper than mere obedience—it touches the heart, it bespeaks the affections. It is a reverence inwoven in the very nature, connected with all the chords of being, and so coming to the surface in obedience and outward respect. We notice—1. That the command is not, "Honor thy father and thy mother *when they do right.*" Our parents, like ourselves, are frail and may commit error. If their error absolved their children from respect, there could be no filial piety in the world. The ground of the command is in the natural relation of the parent, and not in his personal character. We are to honor our parents because they are *parents*, and not because they are saints. Of course this honor will not go so far as to commit or connive at wickedness at their command, for here the other commands of God and the principles of truth modify the commandment in its application. All applications of great truth and divine commands are modified by other great truths and divine commands, as we have seen the command to keep the Sabbath free from ordinary duties is modified by the laws of necessity and mercy. It may become a son's duty to disobey his father because of a command to do evil, or to fasten him with bonds because of insanity; but in every such exceptional case the exception stands boldly out as a testimony to the rule of obedience and respect. While the honor due to parents will not go to wicked or foolish lengths, it *will* go to all reasonable and allowable lengths. It will submit to inconvenience and loss; it will hold its private judgment of what is better in abeyance; it will even keep its own clearly superior wisdom subject to the parental prejudice. So long as conformity to the views and expressed wishes of parents does not harm any third party, a right respect for father and mother will gracefully yield and lay the self-denial on the altar of filial piety.

The same principle teaches a jealous support of the reputation of parents, a readiness to excuse their foibles and mistakes and to set off their virtues against their errors. It will not allow a parent to be ridiculed or denounced without a solemn protest; and if the fault alleged be true, it will go backward and reverentially cover the parent's sin, and so subdue the rebuke.

2. The command is not, "Honor thy father and thy mother *while thou art a little child.*" Many act as if they *had no parents* after they had reached their full stature, and some use this theory even earlier. Now, if to anybody this command is *not* given, it is to the little child, for in his case *nature* and *necessity* teach some degree of obedience and respect to parents, and hence the command is comparatively unnecessary to these. The command comes with peculiar force, and is especially directed, to *children who have entered manhood and womanhood.* They are to remember, in spite of any sense of physical or

mental or social independence, that they are still the children of their parents, and that their parents are their parents still. There is no change in the relationship, only a change in some of the *forms* of its duties. The same honor is due at forty that was due at fourteen. Nowhere is filial reverence more beautiful than when exhibited by a mature and gifted soul. The ancients pictured this in their story of Anchises and Æneas, and the modern Turks and Arabs show their appreciation of this virtue by casting stones at the tomb of Absalom, a prominent example of the opposite vice.

The family is a heavenly institution, and, like the pattern shown to Moses in the mount, has a heavenly meaning in all its relations and relative duties. Woe unto man if he departs from the divine pattern and corrupts the mysterious type! The husband and wife represent Christ and his Church, the parents and offspring represent God and his children, and, above all, the mystic relation of God the Father and God the Son. We only know the mere beginning of the truths that are here recorded in the hieroglyphic of our earthly life. We cannot tell what a vast perversion of truth we may make by the alteration of these symbols, nor can we measure the evil influences and results that such a perversion may have, even though the hieroglyphic be but imperfectly understood. The only safe course for us is that of implicit obedience, a faithful adherence to the celestial organization of the family, in spite of the suggestions of human wisdom, however superior it may boast itself, and in spite of the seductions of a sinful and selfish individuality. When we show all deference and devotion to our parents, we know not what an illustration we may be giving to unseen worlds of the highest truth, and what an emphasis we are adding to the glory of our God. It is this inner connection of our outward domestic life which gives the deep thunder of the death-penalty to the lightning flash of the commandment in the civil polity of Israel. For as the host of God's people stood half on Gerizim and half on Ebal when they took solemn possession of their God-given land, the very second curse uttered before them—the one immediately following the curse upon the worshiper of false gods—was this: "Cursed be he that setteth light by his father or his mother," to which the whole multitude of Israel shouted their responsive "Amen!" and so we find in the inspired code, "He that revileth his father or his mother shall surely be put to death."

It is a Jewish tradition (which bears the marks of authenticity and truth) that the man who was executed for breaking this law of parental regard was denied burial, and his body was cast into the deep, dark valley of Hinnom, into the place called Tophet, where the unclean birds of prey devoured it. It is to this, probably, that

Agur refers when he says, "The eye that mocketh at his father and despiseth to obey his mother, the ravens of the valley shall pick it out and the young eagles shall eat it."

This peculiar severity of punishment marks a peculiar sanctity of the command, which is sustained by the very phrase we constantly use in regard to the virtue enjoined, namely, "filial *piety*." There is nothing, then, to limit the application of the commandment to childhood or youth. The barrier of twenty-one years is a mere human device, useful for some questions pertaining to *human* law, but can have no effect whatever in regard to a *divine* law. The great moral and religious relation of parent and child never ceases. Even when the parent is dead, the parent's memory is to be cherished with reverential affection by the surviving child. This being, then, the purport of God's law issued to every one of us from Sinai, let us—

III. Lastly and briefly ask if there is not *need that God's will in this matter be often rehearsed in our ears.*

As already suggested, I am not disposed to make a special application of this commandment to children. Indeed, in reference to children at all, I would rather urge upon parents *their* duty to see to it that their children are obedient from the earliest infancy. I would say not to little children, "Be obedient to your parents," but rather to parents, "Make your children obedient." It is all in your power. If you indulge your little ones in little irreverences and little disobediences because it looks "so cunning," and foolish friends urge you to the dangerous pastime, then you will have the *little* disobedient children grow to be *big* disobedient children, and they will bring down your gray hairs with sorrow to the grave. Or if, through sheer carelessness and selfish laziness, you avoid the active watchfulness and discipline that are necessary to ensure obedience and to promote an obedient habit, you will obtain the same disastrous result. Beware, too, how, in your anxiety to have your boy a man before the time, you consent to his consequential swagger at sixteen, and furnish him with a night-key as a help to independence, in which you are destroying the bonds of dutiful humility and respectful submission with which God bound him to you at the first, and which God intended you to preserve. It is in this way I would apply the fifth commandment to young children *through their parents*, who are responsible before God and man. I would urge upon them the necessity of bearing ever in mind that obedience with reverential regard is the very rivet which holds the family together, that every other fault can better be tolerated in a child than disobedience or disrespect, and that from this sin spring most legitimately and fruitfully all other forms of filial iniquity and family distress.

But I also make the special application of the text to children of maturer growth—to you who are grown to man's estate, to you who are married and have families of your own, and who have perhaps that rich blessing of God in your house, a grand-mother. Let your continued reverence for your parent or parents still living be of itself a glorious example, deeply written on the thoughts and future memories of your own children. Surround the old age which adorns and honors your household with the tribute of your assiduous care, jealous of its comfort and its dignity, and cover its defects with the mantle (not of your charity, but) of your filial love and sympathy. I have seen an aged father made to act as clerk to his rich son in this city. I have seen an aged mother sent up into a mean garret in order to give room for the young vanities who called her son their father, and you have all seen instances of similar defi-ance to this fundamental family law which

God has stamped on nature as well as published by the writing of his own finger. It is for us, who look to the Lord Jesus in his obedience to his Father as our hope and stay eternal, to regard all such disrespect to parents as we regard theft, falsehood and murder, and to shrink from either the letter or the spirit of a violation of this fifth commandment. Blessed is that house which preserves the beautiful symmetry of the family group as the grapes cluster gracefully about the stem, and where all the domestic virtues find their principle of union and development in their common connection with a pervading filial piety. It is in such a house that we may expect to find the Master as a welcome guest, for there is the spirit of heaven.

The Sixth, Seventh, Eighth and Ninth Commandments.

"*Thou shalt not kill.*
Thou shalt not commit adultery.
Thou shalt not steal.
Thou shalt not bear false witness against thy neighbor."

Exodus xx. 13, 14, 15, 16.

IT must be very noticeable to every reader of the Decalogue that its commands are nearly all prohibitions. There are but two exceptions in the ten—the commandment of the Sabbath and that of respect to parents. All the rest enjoin upon man, not to *perform*, but to abstain. This fact exhibits sin as an ever-acting principle which man is called upon to thwart. This principle acts against God and against our fellow-man, and its cessation of energy can only be founded on a love to God stronger than love to self, and a love to our neighbor equal to the love of self. So when God commands us to cease from sin, he is really bidding us to be holy. By putting his commandments in this form, he is showing us the positive character of our sins, and our true hostility to him while under the sway of sin. He shows us that, so far from imposing a new task upon us, he is only requiring that we should renounce the old tasks which we, as the servants of sin, have assumed; that thus in our differences with him it is *we* that have left him and not *he* that has left us, and that religion is seeking the true by giving up the false—a process which the Scriptures teach us is rendered possible only by the redeeming work of the Lord Jesus Christ.

This method of announcing God's will to man is eminently adapted to bring out into clear relief man's responsibility. It is man who has broken the harmony—it is his to restore it. It is man who has rebelled—it is his to give up his rebellion. His activities are running counter to God's will and law, and in the very nature of the case he must negative this counteraction in order to be at peace with God.

This view of man's condition as a positive sinner summoned to cease his sin, rather than a neutral urged to a positive work, also shows us in very deep colors the wonderful grace of God, which is the more wonderful, not that it comes to help man in an arbitrarily imposed work, but to run after him in his wayward folly and restore him to a position he had forfeited: "God commendeth his love toward us, in that *while we were yet sinners*, Christ died for us."

In examining the ten commandments thus far, we have seen that the first three enjoined a reverence for God in his essence and expression, and the next two enjoined the same reverence by ways promotive of man's highest interests—namely, the observance of God's holy day and respect for parental authority, which is the type and reflection of the divine authority. Through this last we find our way into the commandments which refer exclusively to our duty to man. Of these there are five. The first four we group together. They each read, "*Thou shalt not injure thy fellow-man.*"

We cannot injure *God*—we can only act irreverently and carelessly toward God, and so injure, not him, but ourselves—but our fellow-man we can positively injure, and it is a prime temptation in the race of life to gain on our fellow, not by our diligence, but by thrusting him down. Sin has made us natural enemies to one another, Ishmaelites, whose hands are against every man, and every man's hand against us. The selfish beast who crowds out his neighbor from the crib or even tears him in pieces to destroy his rivalship is but a pattern of man if the restraints of society and providence, from without, be withdrawn.

Man's condition by nature is not seen in man's condition in England, France or civilized America, but in man's condition in the savage island of the Pacific, where the heavenly rays of the gospel have least penetrated. The civilizations of Christianity exhibit, not humanity, but Christianity. The civilizations of ancient Persia, Greece and Rome (although a little revelation filtered through upon them) exhibit humanity, in its best estate, as a refined selfishness, where every man seeks (adroitly, perhaps, and not openly) to injure his neighbor. But even the external refinement of these unchristian civilizations may be traced to that which divine grace has, through its revelation, superimposed upon the sinful race of man. Man, *left to himself*, is the savage, the *cannibal*, the BEAST!

The injury which man can do to his fellow-man can be divided into four kinds—

injury to person, injury to society, injury to property and injury to reputation. The four commandments of the Decalogue in relation to man's injury of man respectively relate to these four forms of human injustice. "Thou shalt not kill" regards any assault on the person; "thou shalt not commit adultery," any assault on society; "thou shalt not steal," any assault on property; and "thou shalt not bear false witness," any assault on reputation. Harm from my fellow-man can reach me only through one of these four channels, and I can *do* harm to another only through the same.

When God surrounded man by the circle of his grace and made him a probationer amid the opportunities of glory, he thereby made man's person sacred. Enough of the image of God was left by the very proximity of this grace to fence around man's person from a violence which would be sacrilege. So we hear God, when Noah and his sons were recommencing the history of the world, declaring, "At the hand of every man's brother will I require the life of man. Whoso sheddeth man's blood, by man shall his blood be shed; for in the image of God made he man." Whatever there was of sanctity in the person of a man was the result of the godly implantation maintained in the conscience by the continual grace of God. When that spark was allowed to be put out, then man's sacredness of person was at an end. The souls that have gone beyond the region of God's long-suffering have no longer a fortified personality. They are left open to the unrestrained attacks of malevolence. A man in hell is unchecked in his aggressions upon others, and no sacredness of person checks aggressions upon himself. There is no law against murder in that lower realm, for the law and the sacredness of the person are both of God, and everything that is godly has withdrawn from the eternal chaos of sin, to dwell for ever among the trophies of the victories of grace. But here upon earth, where grace marks the history of every day, with each of us, in kind providential dealings, in abilities and in opportunities, the human person is sacred and the law against its injury in full and hopeful force. The king's person is called sacred, but God recognizes the person of the humblest peasant to be as sacred as the person of a king, the sacredness being not in the *royalty*, but in the *manhood*, of the man, through grace creative, grace administrative and grace redemptive. It is against such a one that God says, "Do no injury."

"Do not kill" merely marks out the limit of the injury to the person. But it is like a sign-board on the borders of an estate—it includes the whole estate. It embraces in its comprehensive brevity murder in embryo as well as murder in maturity. It points to the *word* and *thought* and *feeling* of murder as well as to the overt *act*. If, in one sense, man is anointed of the Lord, and hence the killing him is sin, it is just as truly sin to *lift up the hand* in threat, to *open the mouth* to revile, or *to think* evil against the Lord's anointed. It is thus that our Saviour interprets this law when he sees denounced in it the "Raca" and the "More"* of the angry man. Our brother man's body is a temple of God, actual or possible, and the respect for that divine temple is to begin in the heart, and by this respect our tendency to ridicule, to despise or to neglect is to be overcome.

By a parity of reasoning, we are not simply to abstain from the overt act of adultery, which irrevocably destroys the ties of family and friendship and makes society a wreck, but the whole field of impurity is to be abandoned by our thoughts. The roots of the crime are to be destroyed as well as the stalk that appears above ground to human observation. It is not that the thought has a tendency to lead to

* "Thou fool" or "thou rebel."

the act, but that the thought is *wrong in itself;* and even if it never go farther, the sin has been committed. It is one of the prominent deceptions of sin to make the outward act the crime, and hence to justify base thoughts and imaginations if they be only confined to the individual mind. But before God the crime is in the immoral position of the heart—a crime which can be exaggerated in its earthly results, but not in its intrinsic viciousness, by a development in action. The very condemnation of the world over whom God sent the deluge was that "every imagination of the thoughts of men's hearts was only evil continually," and the same pure and holy God, who visited those antediluvians first with his grace, and then with his judgment, is he with whom we have to do, who desires "truth in the inward parts" and who recognizes sin as a matter of the heart. Moreover, just as anger is an injury to the person of the object, inasmuch as it degrades and profanes him in our eyes, so impurity is an injury to society, inasmuch as it lowers our estimate of the social bond and weakens it so far as we are concerned.

The position of the heart in each of these cases is a wrong done to our fellow, and in this way we see the true scope of the commandments, to which our Saviour gave no *addition* in his Sermon on the Mount, but only an interpretation. The anger and impurity which he forbade are found in the killing and committing adultery which the law of Sinai forbade. The Sermon on the Mount is only an echo of the Law on the Mount.

Society is sacred because the individual man is sacred; and as there is an image of God in every man, so there is a symbol and type of the heavenly family in human society, and its bonds of blood, affinity and friendship have a divine element in them. Society is no more man-made than is man himself man-made, and he who dares to set at naught its holy bonds in act or in heart is an enemy to God and truth. The man who reads licentious novels, or indulges in lascivious dancing, or countenances the nudities* of so-called art, in life, image or picture, when God made and gave clothes to man and woman, thus sets himself against God and undermines the structure of holiness which God himself has built for our good and his own glory.

The injuries to property and reputation bear a strong analogy to the injuries to the person and society. "Thou shalt not steal" and "Thou shalt not bear false witness" contain the same implication of man's sacredness seen in the murder prohibition. A man's property and reputation are sacred, not because they are property and reputation, but because they are man's property and reputation. Property is the adjunct of a

* The Cupids, Psyches, Apollos, Unas and Venuses, multiplying in our parlors, and becoming more and more wanton in posture and color, show the public preference of Greek heathenism to a chaste Christianity.

man in his own keeping, and reputation is the adjunct of a man in the keeping of society.

Stealing is not wrong as simply inconveniencing our neighbor, as a utilitarian philosophy would teach. An act of theft might never be known to our neighbor, and yet it would be just as much an act of theft as if it had brought him to poverty. It injures our neighbor in his status in our regard and estimation, where he has a right to stand respected and honored. Because he is not aware of the injury, it is no less an injury. I may intercept treasure coming to another, and he never know of the intended gift or of my interference, but I have foully wronged him, nevertheless. It is a crime against the individual man's sacred majesty, and not to be measured at all by visible results. Counting damages is a low, carnal way of reckoning the weight of a crime. It may do for a police regulation in outward society, but it is of no value in the spiritual realm. There the crime has a character in itself outside of any visible consequences. It is branded as *an enmity to God.* So overwhelmingly does this view of the sin press itself upon the fully awakened sinner that a David who has committed adultery and murder, and thus assaulted man socially and personally, cries out, in the bitterness of his anguish of remorse before God, "Against thee, thee only, have I sinned." The harm to man disappears in the insult to God which gives its deepest color to the crime.

It is this innate character of our injury of man which extends the law against theft to all forms of withdrawing or withholding from our neighbor whatever might be rightly counted as his, whether of material estate, of personal ability in body or mind, or of advantages and opportunities. I not only must not take away my neighbor's watch, but I must not stand in the way of the use of his means of personal benefit, I must not lessen his chances of success by adverse processes and I must not encroach unnecessarily upon his time and system. If I prosper by defeating him, as in gambling or mercantile trickery (called shrewdness), I am robbing him. So in regard to his reputation. I am to be judged as much in regard to my silence as my speech concerning him. If I have kept his reputation from growing, by keeping silent when I ought to have spoken for him, I am as much guilty of bearing false witness as if I had opened my mouth in slander. I have not regarded him with that respect with which it became me to regard one made in the image of God. I have done this evil in God's sight and against him.

It is from this view of these commands that we rightly understand our Saviour's declaration that the whole of the second table is summed up in the one spiritual law: "Thou shalt love thy neighbor as thyself." A true love for our fellow-man will alone prevent these four styles of injury.

Love is beneficent, selfishness is malevolent, and there is no neutral ground between them. The love of our neighbor as ourselves regards each man as possessing the same sacred character which we personally possess, and thus makes us jealous for our neighbor's rights and welfare. And this sacred character, as we have seen, is only found in *the image of God* which we bear, so that the whole of the law has one grand foundation, *reverence for God.* This principle, and not any philosophical speculation about natural rights, is the root of the entire ten commandments. So we see in fact that a morality based on natural rights is always a failure, both from the vague definitions of natural rights and the ease with which human lust or ambition will resist and overcome such a motive, while a morality based on regard for God, a reverential love for his holy name, is *never* a failure. This is a *religious* morality, the only one to be trusted.

The whole formula, then, of the law, as

seen through the gospel, is this: "Love God, and love man for God's sake, through Jesus Christ, the God-man."

This is the great argument; but while pressing it, we do not forget that there are many collateral and subordinate arguments, and some low minds need the lower arguments. To one man it is enough to say, "Do not steal, because it dishonors God," but to another you may be obliged to say, "Do not steal, or you will go to prison." The *consequences* to one's self of violating the four commands under consideration are usually treated of in connection with the subject. We are satisfied to pass them by with a word. The murderer, the adulterer, the thief and the liar, even in their beginnings of anger, impurity, acquisitiveness and deceit, are soul-suicides. They are pressing out from their souls all that is divine, obliterating God's image, shaking off the kind fetters of grace, and so removing the very foundation from what remains to them of hope and peace. You who are secretly breaking these commandments in your heart are poisoning your whole moral system. Even if you may be a miser without hurting your neighbor (which we deny), yet you can't be a miser without hurting yourself. The angry man slays himself; the lewd soul pollutes itself; the miser robs himself, and the slanderer destroys his own reputation. There is no resisting the sequence of sin and punishment, except in permitting the interference of divine grace which saves from punishment, and, going farther, saves from sin, which presents the Lord Jesus as the victim for sin and the Holy Ghost as the cleanser *from* sin. Without this divine grace, each one of us must pursue his sins to the bitter end. In Christ pardon and holiness are twin gifts. "The wages of sin is death, but the *gift* of God is eternal life through Jesus Christ our Lord." "Hereby we know that he abideth in us, by the Spirit which he hath *given* us."

THE TENTH COMMANDMENT.

"*Thou shalt not covet thy neighbor's house, thou shalt not covet thy neighbor's wife, nor his man-servant, nor his maid-servant, nor his ox, nor his ass, nor anything that is thy neighbor's.*"—EXODUS XX. 17.

THE ten commandments begin with a demand upon the inmost heart for its true relation toward God, and they end with an appeal to the inmost heart in regard to man's true relation to his fellow. Having given four prohibitions of outward injury toward our neighbor, which legitimately refer to the position of the affections, the Decalogue expressly gathers up the prohibitions into a direct injunction upon the soul. "Thou shalt not covet" prohibits the very source of murder, adultery, theft and slander. In thus closing his law to all men for all time, the Most High shows that a heart-service to man, as to himself, is all that he can recognize as true. He judges not according to any outward appearance, but he looks to the heart. *There* is the individuality, the personality, the *man*.

Here is the fundamental difference between human and divine law. *Human law* has to do with the outward act primarily and principally, and with the motive only secondarily and proximately. It seeks as its ultimates for outward peace, not for inward truth. But the *divine law* deals directly with the motive and heart-principle, and with the outward act only as flowing forth from the motive. Inward truth—"truth in the inward parts," as David expresses it—is the holy and just aim and requirement of the infinitely holy God. Truth, religion, duty (whatever you may call it), is a spiritual matter, and hence the place of obedience and reform is within. "God is a *spirit*, and they that worship him must worship him in spirit and in truth." All attempts at an outward conformity to God's law without the inward life are but the paintings of a corpse into the semblance of life. The clean heart, the new life, is what alone can meet the demands of the Decalogue.

This grand truth, so readily assented to and so readily set aside, is shadowed forth in our own demands of our children. Who of us wishes his children to be obedient automata? Who would be satisfied with a family that went by mechanical machinery? Do we not expect love as the principle in the movements of the household? And if love is found to be wanting in the child, is not his legalistic obedience, his strictness with regard to the letter, almost an offence to us? Can we hold these most proper practical views of earthly relationships, and yet suppose that God can be satisfied with anything less than the heart in *his* children?

The ten commandments, as we see, begin

and end with this view of his fatherly will concerning us, and yet, with strange perversity, men are continually, like the young ruler in the Gospel, quoting this holy law as a "touch-not, taste-not, handle-not" law, to be obeyed by ceremonial exactness or by ascetic precision.

There is a still higher view of this commandment against covetousness than its reference to our inward relation to our fellow-man. The Holy Spirit has himself shown its reference to *our direct relation to God* when he has explained covetousness to be idolatry. In Col. iii. 5 we read: "Mortify, therefore, your members which are upon the earth, fornication, uncleanness, inordinate affection, evil concupiscence, and *covetousness, which is idolatry;*" and again, in Eph. v. 5: "For this ye know, that no whoremonger, nor unclean person, nor *covetous man, who is an idolater*, hath any inheritance in the kingdom of Christ." This last commandment brings us back to the first. We started with God and we end with God. We find that if our true relation with God be maintained, then all other relations will adjust themselves rightly, and that our duty to our neighbor *is founded* on our duty to God. This thought, as taught in God's word, will dissipate any hopes we may have formed from human schemes of philanthropy and social progress. The systems of Fourier and St. Simon have utterly failed, from ignoring the love of God as the source of all philanthropy, supposing that we could be rightly disposed toward our fellow-man without any regard to our relations toward God, or often supposing what was nearly equivalent—that our conduct toward our fellow was the whole of religion. Let us, then, have this lesson deeply impressed upon our hearts from our examinations of God's holy law—that love to man is but an offshoot of love to God, that our relative duties upon earth must derive their worth and efficiency from our positive devotion to our heavenly Father, and that hence the one thing needful for every man is the yielding of his heart to God.

With these thoughts we may proceed more wisely to consider the meaning of the tenth commandment. Let us endeavor to answer four questions: What is coveting? What are the objects which we must not covet? What is the harm of coveting? And, How can we avoid coveting?

I. *What is coveting?* On looking at the Hebrew word here used, "hhamad," we find that it is used of righteous conduct, as for example, in Ps. lxviii. 16: "This is the hill which God desireth (lit., *coveteth*, or hhamad) to dwell in." So in Song of Solomon ii. 3: "I sit down under his shadow with great delight," which is literally, "I *covet* to sit down in his shade." And so the equivalent word in Greek (*ζηλοω*), used by the apostle James in the passages, "Ye kill and desire or *covet* to have," is also used in such passages as these in the first Epistle of Paul to the Corinthians: "Covet to prophesy," "Covet earnestly the best gifts." The Hebrew word is really but expressive of a strong controlling *desire*. Every man has such a desire. The soul is so constituted that it cannot act but through its desires, and one desire must always, from the necessity of the case, be the leader in any particular action. These desires may be *enlightened* through the intelligence and their interrelations thus changed, but they will always remain the springs of life. As a man thinketh or desireth in his heart, so is he, whatever may repress the visible exhibition of his character.

Coveting, then, as simply "ardent desire," is not forbidden *per se* in the commandment, but a special form of coveting, determined by the objects enumerated. The good or evil of a desire is measured by its object and the relations of that object to ourselves. Not by its object alone, for I may desire another man's house; the house is a very good house, but the desire is a very bad desire, because the *relations* of that house to me are such as to condemn the desire. My desire, therefore, as to its goodness or badness, is to be determined by the object *and* its relation to me. Indeed, on close examination, it will be found that nothing (unless it be a rational, moral being itself) is intrinsically bad, that no object which I can desire is in itself evil, that all the bad and the evil is really in the relation it bears to me if I use it or seek it. Prussic acid in itself is not bad—it is just as good as bread or milk; but it would be evil in me to use or seek prussic acid as my food, because its relation to me in that case would be pernicious. We are often confused by words. We apply the words good and bad to *moral* good and evil, and also to mere *physical* properties, and then draw false conclusions from this, which logicians call an "ambiguous middle." Moral good or evil requires a rational responsible agent; the good or evil is in the relation between this rational responsible agent and the object of his desire or use. The good or evil is not in the object, but in me as acting on or toward the object. The coveting, then, in this commandment, having reference to the peculiar relation subsisting between certain objects and ourselves, let us proceed to the second question.

II. *What are the objects which we must not covet?* "Thou shalt not covet thy neighbor's house, thou shalt not covet thy neighbor's wife, nor his man-servant, nor his maid-servant, nor his ox, nor his ass, nor anything that is thy neighbor's."

The special objects here enumerated are not exhaustive, but only representative of a large class. The last clause denotes the wide range from which the enumerated objects are taken as specimens. The house, the wife, the servants, the cattle, represent the four principal departments of a man's earthly establishment—namely, his material possessions, his family, his household and his "live-stock." They illustrate and tend to define the comprehensive phrase, "anything that is thy neighbor's."

It is in this last phrase we particularly trace the answer to our question. If anything belongs to our neighbor, either by the tie of property, as a house, or by the tie of domestic union, as a wife, it thereby partakes of the sacredness of his own person, and is so to be viewed by us. The coveting any such object for ourselves is directly at war with this view. It pollutes this sanctity, it destroys in our heart the harmony of things and introduces confusion. It is against this form of coveting that the command of God lifts itself. Anything appertaining to our neighbor is in such relation to us as to condemn all coveting. The elements of his wealth, his happiness, his fame, his success, are all included. His time, his talents, his opportunities, his advantages, so far as they are peculiarly his and are not common to all, are in the same category.

When we consider that the injury to our neighbor is the basis of the wrong in coveting, and that this injury receives its character from the image of God in man, we can derive the legitimate corollary that we have no right to covet anything which will injure *ourselves;* for God's own compend of the second table of the law is, "Thou shalt love thy neighbor *as thyself.*" Indeed, we can deduce this conclusion in another way, thus: Our health of body and soul is a blessing to our neighbor; it is so much benefit and profit to him; it goes (or should go) to make up the sum of his happiness. Now, then, we have no right to harm that health of body or soul, for then we shall be harming our neighbor. If I covet anything injurious to my own personal efficiency as a member of society, I am plotting against my neighbor, I have begun an attack upon him. What a wide horizon this sweeps! "Thou shalt not covet anything that is thy neighbor's!"

III. *What is the harm of coveting?* The objector may say, "If the coveting goes so far as to become overt crime, I see the harm; but what is the harm of coveting if systematically restrained from outward action, if indulged only in the heart?" The reply is, first, no system can restrain it. You might as well say, "I will put the coal of fire inside the gunpowder-keg and shut it up there tight." But if the supposition could be true, and you could indulge in and cultivate a coveting which would never go farther, there are two directions of evil which even we can detect—God may see a thousand more. We can see, *first*, that *it degrades our neighbor in our hearts.* If he is the object of our hypothetical plunder, he is necessarily lowered in our estimation. But as we have considered this thought in a former chapter, we pass to the *second*, which is—

That we are nursing the brood of sin in our souls. Sins always group together. They are like cowards—one never goes alone. If I allow evil desire a harbor in my heart, my standard of morality will be lowered, I shall grow reckless, shall care less for what is holy and just and good, shall neglect duties generally, and in this way conform my life to the evil desire which, like persistent leaven, will leaven the whole lump. The human heart and life is like the exquisite machinery of a watch. If you put one wheel off its axis, you derange the whole working. You cannot be sinful in one part only of the soul; man's life is an ultimate unit, and has no parts. We talk of the different *parts* of a man's mind, but this is a language used to assist our feeble comprehension. Sin in the *desire* is sin in the *man*—the *entire* man; so that the harm done by coveting what is not our own is just the harm done by *sin* when welcomed to the heart. It is spiritual corruption—gangrene. You can hide it from human observation, but that does not stop the inner destruction for a moment. You are carefully cherishing the eggs of envy, jealousy, malice, anger and revenge, when you indulge in your unhallowed desires; and these dire monsters will be hatched and become your irresistible masters before you are aware. How pressing, then, our fourth question!

IV. *How shall we avoid this evil coveting?* Will any mere order from the intelligence be heeded by the wild desire? Or can any magic power be invoked to slay the desire and save the man? Full of depravity, which is seen first in these wicked desires of the heart, we listen hopefully to God's word sent to us by his saving love: "Set your affection on things above, not on things on the earth." Here is the wisdom from above, the philosophy of heaven. The desires of the heart are not to be annihilated, man is not to be reduced to an inert lump, his passions are to burn as brightly as ever, his eager heart to beat as strongly, his eye to sparkle with anticipation and his energies to leap as actively as before, yet not for worldly jewels, but for heaven's crown. The current is to run as swiftly as before, but now in a *new channel.* We are to seek *first*—that is, as *chief*—the kingdom of God and his righteousness.

This glorious specific, this complete remedy, may have either a special or a general application. A man may find a single evil desire temporarily affecting him. With a Christian heart he remembers that his Redeemer is ever at hand. He calls out in the agony of his self-reproach amid the perplexity of his divided soul; and in turning to his Saviour, his affections are withdrawn from the passing evil and restored to their healthy channel. The contemplation of Jesus is the application of a magnet to attract the desires of his soul. This is a frequent experience of the renewed, and gives peculiar lustre to the words of the apostle, "Looking unto Jesus."

It is this remedy which awaits the use of you who are disturbed because of your worldly longings. You are writing bitter things against yourselves, and feel almost ready to despair of Christian attainment. The great truth should be understood by you that you will never cease to have these worldly longings until Christ becomes so lovely in some forms of his character or work as to draw off these energies of desire from their unworthy channel. Overcome every special worldliness by a special heavenly contemplation. And so, *generally*, let me assure the unconverted that their depraved desires will never cease until holy desires take their place. "Thou shalt not covet thy neighbor's," can never be obeyed until you learn to covet your own—those blessed gifts of heavenly grace which God urges upon you, and which properly belong to you. Each of you, my unregenerate readers, is to be renewed, if at all, by taking these very desires which are now bounding after the world and turning them to the Lord Jesus. You see at once that it will be an *act* on your part, an *effort*, but an act and effort that will save your soul. Is not the act worth taking? Is it not perilous to postpone the effort? The Lord is waiting for your reply.

In our examination of the Decalogue we have especially noted the following points:

I. That it is God's law for all men of all ages.

II. That none can appreciate it and obey it but those who have been saved by divine grace.

III. That it is eminently and intensely a spiritual law, demanding truth in the inward parts.

IV. That it teaches us directly to honor God in his essence and expression (avoiding a false expression and using the true with deep reverence), and to honor our fellow-man as bearing the image of God, avoiding his injury in either act, thought or feeling, and that it is thus summed up by the formula: "Thou shalt love the Lord thy God with all thy heart, and thy neighbor as thyself."

We thus see that the gospel is not antagonistic to the law, but a divine way for us to keep the law, and that while the gospel saves, in the very act of saving us it gives us the law as our rule of life—that holy law which God never intended to become obsolete, but which reflects his own holiness and is as eternal as is God himself. Do you love that law? There is no better proof of your salvation. Do you *not* love it? Then go to Jesus, that he may teach you how to love it by teaching you how TO LOVE HIM.

www.ingramcontent.com/pod-product-compliance
Lightning Source LLC
LaVergne TN
LVHW021402110826
845150LV00007B/1748

* 9 7 8 1 4 2 5 5 1 3 0 2 3 *